9780910386951
AF593383

To Lucy, who has endeavored over the years to put cities in perspective.

The exhibition is made possible by grants from

The Cleveland Foundation, The East Ohio Gas Company, and the Ohio Arts Council

CERVIN ROBINSON

CLEVELAND, OHIO

An exhibition of 100 photographs commissioned by The Cleveland Museum of Art

Photographs and Introduction by Cervin Robinson with a Foreword by Evan H. Turner

PUBLISHED BY THE CLEVELAND MUSEUM OF ART IN COOPERATION WITH INDIANA UNIVERSITY PRESS

Cover: Rockefeller Building. Superior Avenue at West 6th Street. 1905. Knox and Elliott, architects and designers; ornamental ironwork cast by Winslow Brothers Foundry. October 1987.

All photographs are gelatin silver prints, taken between July 1987 and April 1988.

Library of Congress Cataloging-in-Publication Data
Robinson, Cervin
Cervin Robinson Cleveland, Ohio.
p. cm.
Catalogue of an exhibition commissioned by the Cleveland Museum of Art.
ISBN 0-910386-98-6 (pbk.). ISBN 0-910386-99-8.
1. Photography, Architectural—Exhibitions. 2. Robinson, Cervin—Exhibitions. I. Cleveland Museum of Art. II. Title.
TR659.R6247 1989
779'.4' 092—dc20 89-22050
CIP

Distributed by Indiana University Press, Bloomington, Indiana
Publication staff: Laurence Channing, Sally W. Goodfellow, Emily S. Rosen, and Jo Zuppan
Printed by Meriden-Stinehour Press, Lunenberg, Vermont
Typesetting by Live Publishing, Inc., Cleveland, Ohio

Contents

Foreword

Each city has its particular character—and certainly Cleveland is no exception to such a generalization. That character, in part, is an expression of its inhabitants; for example, their ethnic origin and subsequent assimilation, their means, and their moral values (few cities of comparable size, one suspects, have as many places of worship scattered among its neighborhoods as Cleveland). But that sense of a city's character is also greatly affected by the pattern of streets emerging over the years in response to the community's evolving needs and by the buildings, put up by successive generations, that remain standing. The 100 images published here and simultaneously exhibited at The Cleveland Museum of Art present a broad overview of this northeastern Ohio city by a distinguished American architectural photographer, Cervin Robinson.

The photographs in the aggregate are not intended to be an architectural history or record of Cleveland. Knowingly, major buildings are omitted, and others are only seen in part. Such early buildings as Dunham Tavern (1824), the "Old Stone Church" (1858), and at 3813 Euclid Avenue the Beckwith mansion (1852) are not to be found at all. Instead the photographs should be viewed as one individual's considered effort to grasp the particular character of a major American city as a whole. It is the dynamics existing between buildings (more often by chance than intent), the juxtaposition of the grandiloquent and the simple, the fascination of details (at times more distinguished than the building as a whole), all seen in the shifting light of the various seasons—such are the factors to be considered in an architectural appraisal of a city. At times the subjects chosen will come as no surprise—although quickly one will recognize that the vision behind the image is unique—at other times the choice of subject may be startling or even, possibly, felt to be negative in spirit. However, as satisfying as the individual images may be, the success of a photographic essay such as this can only be properly gauged when the material is pondered as a whole.

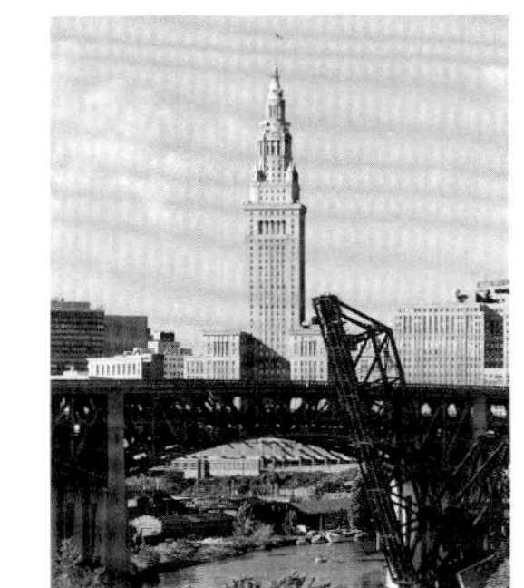

The photographs are about Cleveland's streets and buildings. They are meant to challenge those who live in Cleveland. In the exhibition itself no image is in fact identified—instead the titles appear at the end of the installation. This is done deliberately, to encourage visitors to draw upon their own experiences of the city and to nurture in each an individual sense of recall. Studying Cervin Robinson's photographs will encourage all to look at the city with new perspectives—and, hopefully, with a increased sense of responsibility. However, the exhibition is equally important for those who may only know Cleveland fleetingly, for the presentation of a thoughtful point of view on one city can provoke a similar consideration of any major urban center with great profit.

It may be useful to identify certain key factors in a broad overview of Cleveland's history, to assist in placing Cervin Robinson's remarkable photographs as well as the interesting perceptions of his introduction in a larger context.

In 1796 surveyors for the Connecticut Land Company, led by Moses Cleaveland, arrived at the point where the meandering Cuyahoga River runs into Lake Erie in the further reaches of the Western Reserve (the 3 million acres that had been reserved to Connecticut when the Northwest Territory was established). In less than four months they drew up a plan for the ideal New England community which was expected with time to attract settlers to the river's east bank; the west bank was still in Indian hands. The plan, centering upon a ten-acre public square surrounded by parallel streets, remains to this day the heart of downtown Cleveland. The exception to the rectilinear grid—the diagonal Euclid Avenue—follows an earlier Indian trail from the east.

Numbers of people did indeed move from the Connecticut River Valley to the lands of the Western Reserve, but few came as far west as Cleveland. Although the site augured well for the future, the low-lying river nurtured insects while the winds sweeping across the lake from the west made the winters harsh. For the next twenty-five years the settlement remained little more than a small pioneer village, while other communities in the Western Reserve thrived.

The opening of the Erie Canal in 1825, however, changed this, as it completed the link between New York City and Lake Erie, thereby providing would-be settlers with an easy and inexpensive approach. The canal boom was on, and the state began constructing the Ohio Canal with Cleveland as its northern terminus. Reaching as far as Akron by 1827, it connected Cleveland with the Ohio River by 1832. Thus, the first major step was taken in establishing the city's future prosperity. With the exception of eight miles of portage at Akron, the canal linked Cleveland with New Orleans via a continuous inland waterway, giving Ohio's farmers easy access to profitable markets. As canal traffic burgeoned, Cleveland also became a major port in the active trade developing on the Great Lakes. The wide valley of the Cuyahoga River near its mouth—now called the "Flats"—was soon lined with docks and the associated warehouses next to them and on the land above. That Cleveland prospered is evident in its growth, from just over 600 residents in 1825 to a population of more than 8,000 in 1854 when Cleveland united with its eager competitor, Ohio City, which had developed to the west of the river.

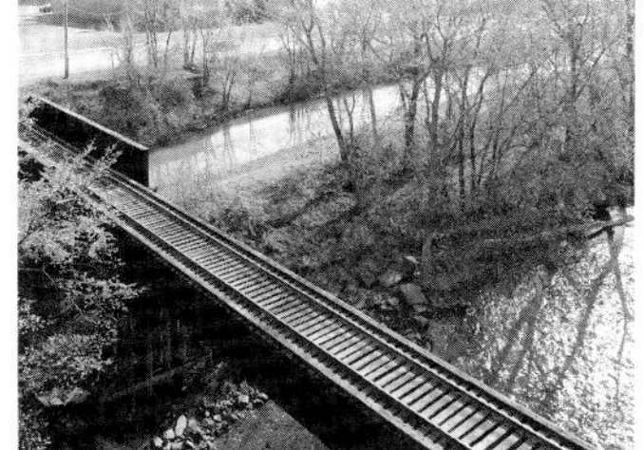

Canals brought success, but the railway had an even greater impact upon the city's prosperity. It arrived by midcentury and a decade later the state of Ohio led the nation in the number of miles of railway track. To attract the various lines, Cleveland gave away such rights as those to the prime property along the lake (thereby stifling civic efforts to take appropriate advantage of the city's shoreline for many years to come). The railway brought coal from Pennsylvania and West Virginia even as the rapidly expanding fleet of lake ships brought iron ore from the Lake Superior region to the north. Mills and factories were rapidly constructed as close to the river as possible to take advantage of this. In the last quarter of the nineteenth century Cleveland was a remarkably prosperous manufacturing center, but the associated industrial pollution became an enduring problem.

The city's population expanded rapidly, in part because the new mills needed large numbers of workers. Groups of immigrants from various European countries, from Wales and Ireland as well as Germany, Czechoslovakia, and other southeastern European countries, filled that need. That these immigrants tended to come as groups helps in understanding Cleveland today. Upon arrival, each group established its own community, adjacent to the mills, which constructed rows of simple houses for their use. Usually the homogeneous characters of the neighborhoods were nurtured, and their native languages were preferred over English within the neighborhood. Once established, a grand church symbolic of immigrant aspirations would be constructed; at times its decoration evoked traditions left at home. Today, these diverse ethnic communities remain one of the most vital factors in the city's life.

Little is left of pre-Civil War Cleveland, but this is hardly surprising. In the second half of the nineteenth century, commerce came first. There was little time for proper civic planning; all efforts were invested in dealing with industrialization and technological advances—such as the telegraph—which occurred with a speed well beyond the city's control. Buildings were put up in response to the community's basic needs—whether domestic, religious, educational, or administrative—but then those buildings were torn down and quickly replaced by more ambitious ones. In the last years of the nineteenth century, however, the city constructed several buildings whose Romanesque grandeur, reflecting the influence of Henry Hobson Richardson, make them some of the finest buildings still standing. Churches sprang up as well in all areas. Frequently today their splendor in neighborhoods that have since declined proclaim the moment of affluence.

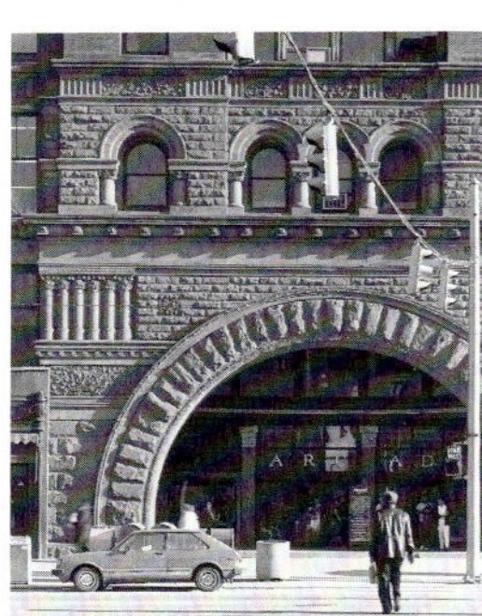

The one constant was the city's original ground plan. Scarcely appropriate to the topography at the outset, it became only more impractical, but the rectilinear grid remained dominant until the middle of the century. As the city's numbers skyrocketed and as the middle class expanded, however, new neighborhoods and patterns of streets were established, on the East Side beyond 55th Street and on the West Side. Gracious houses surrounded by expansive lawns lined Euclid Avenue; they were often as grand as they were eccentric. Alas, as factories multiplied and, probably even more important, as the railway crossed Euclid Avenue at East 55th Street, even they succumbed to the vengeance of progress. In the late nineteenth century grandeur was concentrated increasingly around the most important new public park established since Public Square, lying adjacent to East 105th Street. Even today Wade Park (1882) perpetuates the name of its original donor, Jeptha Wade. Gradually, however, thanks to a rapidly expanding new system of electric street railways, residential splendor crept up Cedar Road Hill— the northern edge of the Appalachian Plateau—to the new neighborhood of Cleveland Heights and out along the lake shore to Bratenahl.

By 1900 the city which fifty years earlier had had about 8,000 residents had grown to about 382,000—larger by a few thousand than Cincinnati, Buffalo, and Pittsburgh, yet much smaller than the 1,698,000 of Chicago. Nonetheless, it was the seventh most populous of America's cities, and the city prospered. The presence of the steel industry gave Cleveland an advantage with the new automotive industry— with impressive results. The founding and subsequent growth of the Standard Oil Company (1870) introduced a major new source of prosperity, and it remains today an important factor in the life of the city. Understandably, Cleveland was generally regarded as one of America's most promising industrial and commercial centers at the start of the twentieth century.

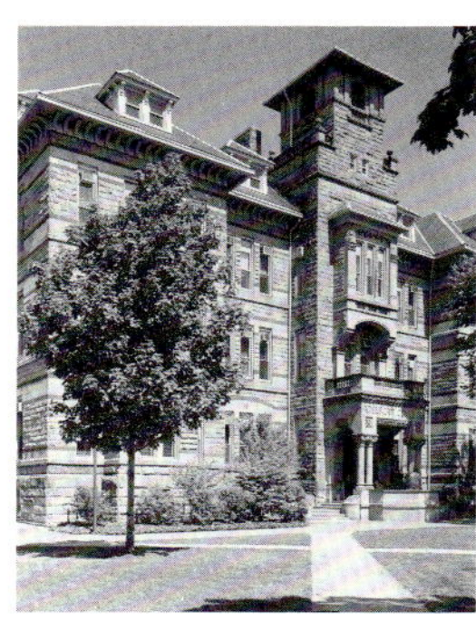

Prosperity well established, a sense of greater community responsibility gradually emerged. Developing Cleveland as the area's major educational resource was given a high priority. Western Reserve College, founded at Hudson in 1826, was moved to land adjacent to Wade Park in 1882 near the new Case School of Applied Science, where united as one, the two continue today. Thus Cleveland put in place the other most significant factor in the city's plan, a great center of learning meant to balance the commercial area centered on downtown's Public Square. Euclid Avenue, which was lined with the residences of those who made it all possible, linked the two areas.

Nearby yet another major piece of parkland was established thanks to the generosity of John D. Rockefeller. This picturesque drive along Doan Creek, which connected Wade Park with the lake, became the setting for a series of gardens honoring the city's various cultural communities.

Before the close of the nineteenth century, a relatively small group of affluent citizens, who had the foresight to recognize not only that Cleveland must match the example of other major American cities but also that there was an obligation to those who had made the city's success a reality, took the initial steps towards establishing cultural institutions for the city. The construction around Wade Park of the various suitable buildings was one significant accomplishment of the first quarter of the new century.

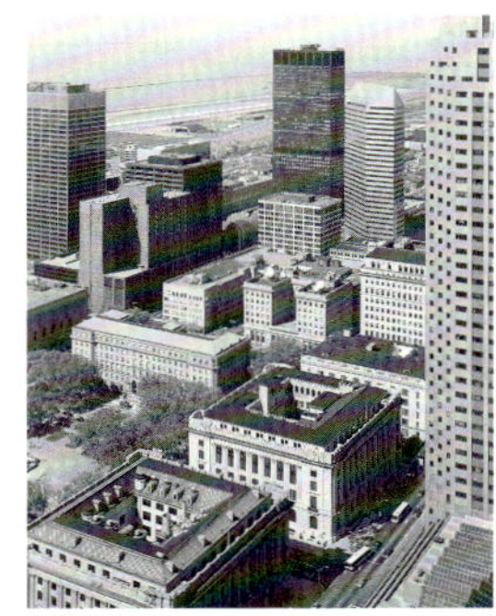

Simultaneously the city's leaders recognized the need for introducing some semblance of order in the downtown chaos. Finding some resolution for this concern absorbed them for the years to come. The various buildings scattered here and there before and after the Civil War to satisfy the city's judicial and civil needs were no longer practical or even appropriate for a thriving metropolis. Thus in 1902, much impressed by the stylistic unity of Daniel Burnham's plan for the 1893 Columbian Exposition in Chicago, the city's leaders commissioned a group led by Burnham to find a similar solution for Cleveland. No American city had commissioned such a plan since L'Enfant laid out Washington at the end of the eighteenth century. The group conceived a great Mall overlooking the lake. Land was cleared and a grand urban space was created, around which were constructed the Federal Building (1910), the City Hall (1916), the County Court House (1911), the Public Auditorium (1922), the Public Library (1925), and the Board of Education Administration building (1930). A flurry of construction also resulted in various bank buildings whose elegance rivalled that of their neighbors on the Mall.

Even as the needs of the city politic were resolved, the ambitious and ingenious vision of the Van Sweringen brothers came to fruition at the southwest corner of Public Square, with the construction of the Terminal Tower complex. Viewed as a city within a city, the Union Terminal Group included a hotel, office buildings, a department store, shops, and banks. All, most significantly, were situated over a huge railroad station where the national east-west railroad lines crossed a network of local rapid transit lines connecting the downtown with a new neighborhood built on Van Sweringen lands just beyond Cleveland Heights. Known as Shaker Heights, the area took shape during the 1920s and the 1930s. It enjoyed a remarkable stylistic unity because of a strict building code established by the brothers. Far removed from the city's industry, this area, with twisting roads and verdant yards, could be seen as the utopian neighborhood that had been a national dream since the earliest years of the new nation.

The Depression years were hard ones—little was constructed in Cleveland although there was a considerable amount of dreaming. In some ways this hiatus—which continued in the 1940s, when Cleveland was deeply involved in the war effort (which meant another major influx of labor, this time from the American South)—may be said to have had its advantages. Had it been otherwise, even more of the earlier buildings might well have been torn down and replaced by the monotonous forms that were too often constructed during those years. This moratorium on construction had another important impact upon the appearance of the city. Older buildings were remodeled to respond to new needs; frequently one building of an earlier group was torn down to make way for an incongruous addition on another. But such is the fate of the modern American city, as well as a significant factor in its character.

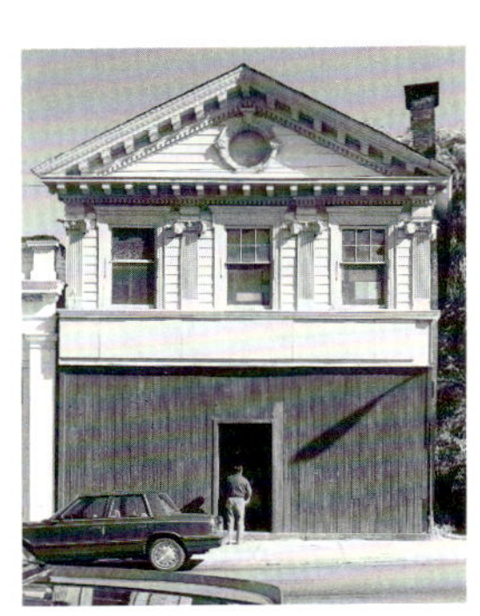

After World War II, Cleveland's ambitious plans were in many ways characteristic of those found in other American cities. Great office towers were constructed downtown, notably around East 9th Street. Once again transportation had a major impact upon the city. A network of new highways linking the heart of the downtown with the interstate system, swept through neighborhoods, even as a new transit system was created on existing tracks to connect the city and its suburbs with the airport.

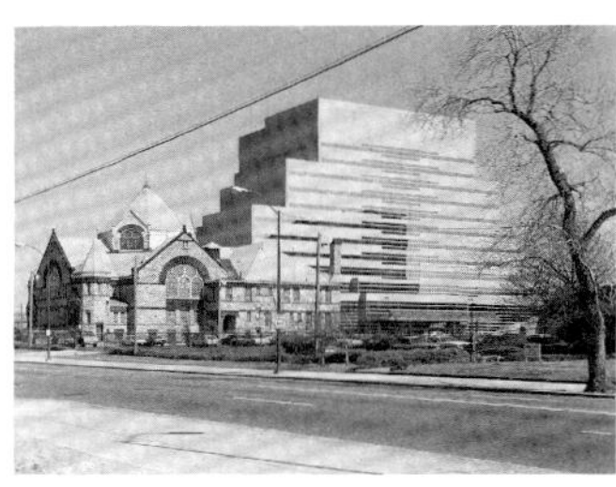

In the last decade Cleveland has faced yet again new challenges and done so in a characteristic manner. The city's economic base has changed radically. No longer a leading manufacturing center, it now finds strength in its service economy. Hospitals are the major employers, and they display the same ambitious building plans evident in the earlier construction of factories. Finally, downtown Cleveland is cleaner and the sense of urban responsibility characteristic of the city at the turn of the century becomes increasingly responsive to citizen needs. The lower Cuyahoga River Valley, the so-called "Flats," left essentially vacant by the departure of industry, gradually emerged as a recreational haven even as serious efforts were made to take advantage of the lake front. The greening of Public Square has become a major concern even as ambitious new plans for construction on its periphery are launched.

An undertaking as complicated as this exhibition has inevitably involved great numbers of people. Everyone, we've discovered, has a favorite view or an unknown corner which would be an appropriate subject. More people have made interesting suggestions than could ever be properly thanked: William D. Ginn epitomizes such help. Let it be said only that such widespread interest in the project augurs well for Cleveland's future.

Timothy H. Barrett, formerly of the Western Reserve Historical Society, not only shared information but introduced Cervin Robinson to the city's neighborhood churches. Karen Horn arranged introductions to areas not readily open to the public, as did Lucy Ireland, Thomas W. Morris, R. Henry Norweb, Jr., Judith Salomon, Mrs. Alfred L. Williams, and William G. Hachtel.

Commissioning a New Yorker of New England origins, a man who is almost as knowledgeable about the history of architectural photography as he is distinguished as an artist, has the great advantage of choosing one who considers Cleveland free of the many associations inevitably experienced by a resident of the city; however, there is the disadvantage of his having to accumulate a considerable amount of information about the city in a relatively short time. Many have helped. The Director of the Western Reserve Historical Society, Theodore Anton Sande, shared information with his usual generous spirit, while his colleague Eric Johannesen, through his publications as well as discussions, proved invaluable in nurturing some understanding of Cleveland's ethnic communities which are as complicated as, certainly, they are fascinating. The architect, Peter van Dijk, who has contributed a great deal to the quality of Cleveland's urban scene, generously shared his love and knowledge of the city, as did Walter S. Gibson.

In New York various people helped: Judith and Joel Herschman, Ned Polsky, Mark Wright, Sam Robinson, and particularly Cervin Robinson's former assistant, Elizabeth Feeley.

At The Cleveland Museum of Art, the Museum's Curator of Contemporary Art, Tom Hinson, is responsible for the exhibition and worked closely with Cervin Robinson on its installation. Lynn Cameron handled the myriad numbers of details in connection with the photographer's various trips to Cleveland, while at times Julie Bush provided able assistance on the job. The Museum's Head of Publications, Laurence Channing, has devoted many hours to the design of the publication, intriguing hours since the juxtaposition of images can have such a great impact upon the ideas lurking in each one.

In the final analysis, however, two Cleveland people and two Cleveland institutions have been focal to the realization of this undertaking. The Cleveland Foundation and The East Ohio Gas Company equally provided the funds which made it possible for the Art Museum to award this commission. We are deeply appreciative.

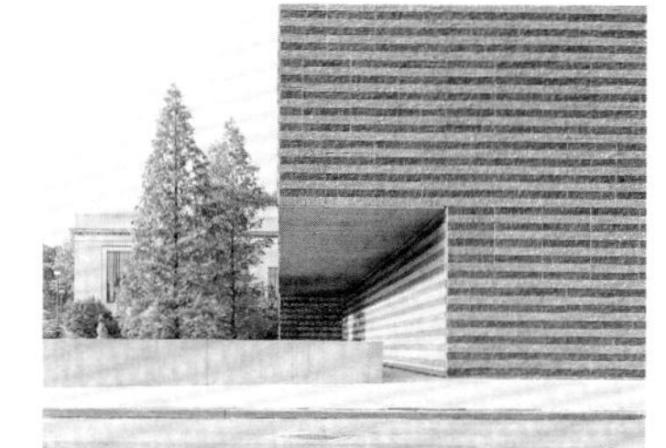

In carrying it out, Cervin Robinson visited the city eight times in order to take full advantage of seasonal changes. At the outset he went to Cleveland's Assistant Director of the City Planning Commission, Edward A. Reich, and as Clevelanders have repeatedly discovered over the years, Ned was invaluable in suggesting lively possibilities and ferreting out hard-to-find information. Holly Rarick has spent many hours researching the dates, the architects, and the proper names of the many buildings photographed, thereby making this publication an invaluable resource for the future.

That such a perceptive photographer of the urban scene as Cervin Robinson should have been commissioned to undertake this study of Cleveland today, may properly be recognized as one manifestation of the city's renewed concern for its future. Because the example of the past— successes as well as failures—should not be overlooked as the city plans for the future.

E. H. T.

Introduction

What can photography possibly say about the essential character of Cleveland and its citizenry? The camera has a mind of its own—built-in preferences as to what it wants to show and boundaries to what it can show. Photographs of any city, whether taken by a native or an outsider, are inevitably both attempts to respond to an order already in the city and to impose a plausible order, one partly inherent in the nature of the camera.

Photographs can show only what is skin deep. They talk about externals, and therefore if pictures are to have a sense of history, subjects must be seen as time has marked them. Clean up a building cosmetically and it will no longer be worth photographing, at least not in the way it was before.

Photographing something, even the familiar—perhaps particularly the familiar—is not recording it as it looks but finding out how it looks in a picture. And bringing together a set of pictures all taken from the same point of view and in the same light can mean creating the illusion of a community that has never existed except in these photographs.

A pair of buildings in a single photograph will seem engaged in a dialogue that will charge the picture with meaning in the same way that subjects of adjacent photographs acquire linked meanings (and a taste for such photographs will develop in a viewer a sensitivity to the urban dialogues they depict). A similar dialogue will take place between a building and a tree juxtaposed to it. Indeed telephone poles and lamp posts will serve the same function. Trees will suggest that a building is good; telephone poles and lamp posts, representing ugly reality, will suggest objectivity, so the meanings of the juxtapositions are different. Even the search for subjects can change a photographer's attitute towards them: if he hunts for examples of something he means to criticize—for instance of the Greek Revival for the awkwardness it seemed at one time to have or of the Victorian for the ugliness once seen in it—he will develop a taste for his subjects. They will have become picturesque.

The pictures we choose to take are in part determined by memories and by habits. We carry with us the memories of pictures that have mattered to us just as writers carry the memories of books that have mattered to them. A photographer in the Depression years could model his pictures on those of the American Civil War. I bring to Cleveland the memory of views of the 1930s—or even of engravings of eighteenth-century Rome. In New York, where I started to photograph architecture, one learns to excise with the camera sections of buildings small enough to show with clarity architectural detail yet large enough to suggest the mass of the largest structures. If I had learned to photograph in a town of small, wood-framed buildings, I would have, not that, but some other skill. I would not be entirely surprised if someone said I had turned Cleveland into a kind of New York, though I do not think I have done so.

If a large part of photographing is knowing what the camera does well, another is attempting to show subjects as one experiences them. As well as being a hired gun, I believe in cities and have always chosen to live in one or another of them. Like any traveller I want a city other than my own to be different, even exotic. At the same time I mean to find the key to how an alien city is used and to discover its essential character. Like a traveller with a guide book I want to identify the buildings that I will have occasion to use (hotel, post office, museum, etc.) and the buildings that, while I may not use them, are essential to any city (city hall, school, library, apartment block, etc.). Formerly the first list would certainly have included a railway station and might have included a cathedral—indeed towns have been summed up in terms of the cathedrals that dominated them. In our time the county courthouse has seemed sufficiently emblematic to form the basis for a study of America and its architecture.[1]

If there is neither a single emblematic building nor even a set of buildings in which Cleveland can be summed up, perhaps photographs can demonstrate the following: Cleveland is a city on Lake Erie at the point where the Cuyahoga River enters it. Structures of heavy industry, notably in the form of steel mills, line either bank of the river, but most signs of a canal that once connected Lake Erie to the Ohio River have disappeared. On high ground directly above this valley, just to the north of the river before it finally turns to the lake, is Cleveland's downtown, centered on Public Square. To one side of this square is a group of Beaux-Arts city, county, and federal buildings, and beyond that a street of curtain-walled office buildings built since World War II. Adjacent to these groups on the side nearer the river are a district of older warehouse buildings, and on the side away from it an area of stores, office buildings, banks and theaters. On other high ground above the river to the west and south are neighborhoods founded to house workers for the mills, the most remarkable being a district called Tremont, whose church steeples punctuate the drive into the city from Cleveland's major airport. To the east of downtown is an area left in disarray by changing uses and demolition; beyond that are a group of medical, cultural, religious, and educational institutions on or near parkland, above which in turn are handsome and famous suburbs above a bluff.

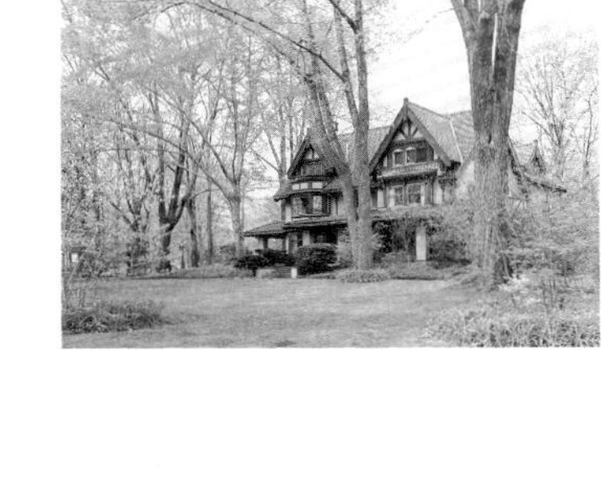

To what extent can one show this in photographs? Two different answers are possible. One answer is that it is the photographer's job to describe whatever exists; the other is that his job is to seek out only what is visually articulate. The first answer suggests that photographers should apply themselves precisely where the old formulas no longer work, where the new dimensions of a modern city (largely introduced by the automobile) and new architectural solutions defy them. Indeed, rumors to the contrary, contemporary architecture is not directed by a sense of what will photograph gracefully. In their current work in New York City Cesar Pelli and Associates and Kohn Pedersen Fox, two architectural firms also active in Cleveland,[2] have made the point that their buildings can respond directly to older buildings that are not immediate neighbors, that are in fact out of sight. How can one photograph that? The second answer sees the city as essentially a dense, ordered, pedestrian phenomenon readily described by the camera except where it has been destroyed by the automobile, popular as that destruction has been, or by the real estate speculator and his greed.

A camera turned to the lakefront will demonstrate that Cleveland has relegated to its waterfront the sorts of uses most American cities have thought it appropriate to relegate to theirs: a multilane highway, parking fields, a municipal airport, a stadium, railway tracks. Though the lake appears in pictures of the city's downtown, no dialogue is apparent and the lake therefore passes almost unnoticed. But the lake's significance for the city is apparent in photographs of the eastern, lakeside suburb of Bratenahl, where the meeting can be found celebrated architecturally; the west end of the city at Rocky River, where there is a nautical link; nearer downtown in Lakewood, where apartment slabs almost directly abut the water; or still farther in where Hulett unloaders wait at the water's edge.

Indeed, a clearly visible, abrupt transition, whether designed by an architect or impelled by necessity is usually an urban virtue and one that photographs well, especially when emphasized by topography.

1. *Courthouse: A Photographic Document*, Richard Pare, ed. (New York: Horizon Press, 1978).

2. Neither is a Cleveland firm but Robert Evans, one of the two design partners responsible for KPF's AmeriTrust Center, is a native of Cleveland.

The sharp transition between downtown Cleveland on its heights and the industrial flats in their valley below—the juxtaposition emphasized by tall buildings on the high ground and low buildings beneath—has long been the city's most compelling image. On the opposite side of the valley it is reflected more faintly in the juxtaposition of these same flats to Tremont with its church domes and spires. It is where such appositions are direct and unblurred that the camera can describe them clearly. It is therefore some seven miles inland where river, railroad, and roadway come closest to a remaining fragment of the Ohio and Erie Canal that the canal can still be photographed juxtaposed to the river, which fed it, the railway, which made it obsolete, and the roadway, which has largely superseded the railway.

Within the downtown itself transitions that can be seen as dialogues were designed into individual buildings and also occur between neighbors or neighboring groups of buildings. Where they are found in a single facade, as in the Sullivan-like massing and crystalline decorative scheme of the Rockefeller building, or occur between buildings abutting side by side, the camera's head-on perspective so resembles the architect's elevation that its response is simple and appropriate, urban virtue translated directly into photographic terms.

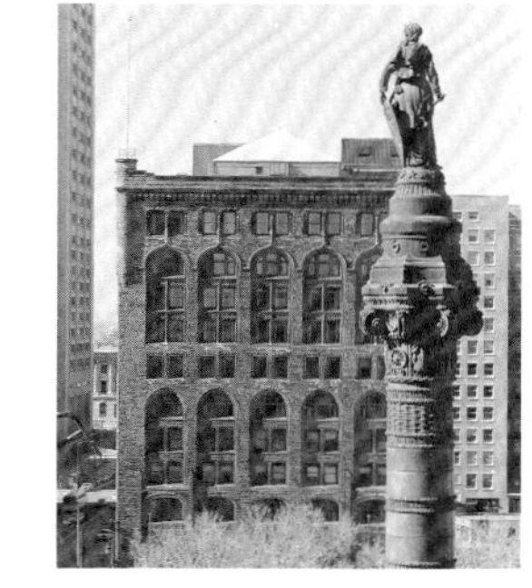

Other urban experiences are less directly transferable. The center of the city is Public Square, and the buildings that surround it are engaged in dialogue with one another. Of these buildings the anchor is not the oldest or the newest or the tallest, but a Chicago skyscraper of the late 1880s that enjoys this role because of its rough vigor and because its mass is brought down to the scale of the sidewalk by a lamp at its corner supported by a wrought-iron vine (the tree of life or the tree of knowledge?). Traffic lights and parking signs spoil the corners of many blocks in America. Here they prevent this lamp from being photographed properly.

The dialogue of buildings across a square is less accessible to photography than is that of two buildings side by side; when the camera faces one, it has the other behind it. However, in Public Square the column surmounted by a statue of *Liberty* above the Soldiers and Sailors Monument can act with the bank as an interlocutor in a photographic dialogue. The bank itself plays a more complex role in downtown Cleveland: it stands for a model of the urban office building (craggy and primitive) that is at variance with the alternative offered by the refined, urban, polite, and European buildings of the neighboring Group Plan. An alternative to photographing the bank with the monument is its juxtaposition to the Beaux-Arts County Courthouse that ends the Ontario Street axis of Public Square. The two pictures are close enough to require a choice between them, and the one with the column is the better picture.

Photographing downtown is only rarely a matter of directly recording experience; it is instead a matter of stitching parts of the fabric together as one can. Although the tops of the two tall buildings on Public Square, the Terminal Tower and the BP Building, dominate the skyline, they cannot be shown in dialogue across the square; but the first can be shown from a block north of the square in juxtaposition to each of two worthy buildings on St. Clair Avenue. The second, because its designers have linked it both to Public Square and to an axis of the Group Plan (and because that axis has been celebrated by a fountain and a sculptural figure), can be shown juxtaposed to the Federal Building and the Public Library.

After the Second World War curtain-walled office towers collected along East 9th Street, just as did similar buildings along Park Avenue in New York, and, as in New York, because they were imagined largely in isolation these modern buildings had little relationship to one another and even less relationship to their older neighbors, which it was believed would themselves soon be replaced by other modern buildings. It is characteristically as reflected in another's curtain wall that one of these buildings can be shown in its environment.

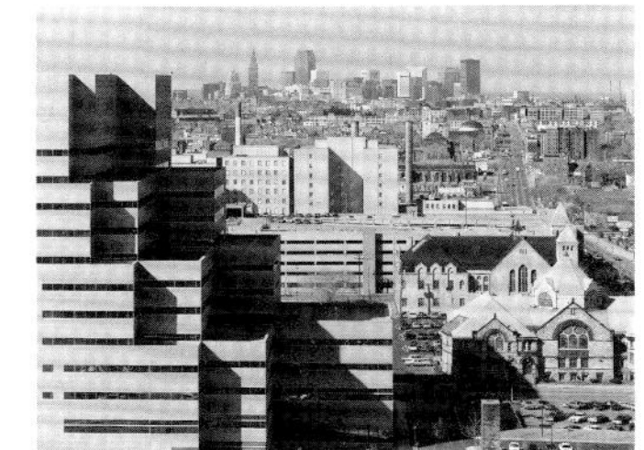

Photographs can show only to a limited extent the fragmented nature of the area east of the city center, but the area can be summed up by a view back towards the center from the neighborhood of the Cleveland Clinic (but, incidentally, only at the price of showing one of the clinic's newer buildings in what its designer would consider an unflattering light, i.e., with black slots for windows in place of a continuous, taut skin of wall). Farther east dialogues pick up between the monumental buildings of the University Circle and Wade Park area, where structures again relate to each other articulately.

Unlike the dramatic change in elevation between the flats and downtown Cleveland, the abrupt change in elevation between the university area and the suburbs above is blurred by vegetation. In an automobile one experiences the change, but there is no visual expression of what happens—no Spanish Steps to celebrate the topographic event. As it penetrates the suburbs above, the camera can show only components one by one, not the sequences one experiences from a moving car. Where the automobile dominates, the camera can at best take pictures of elements that may cause us to recall our past experiences, but the relationship of the parts is lost. On the road from the airport into the city one travels at still higher speeds, and the disparity between the experience of orbiting church steeples in and near Tremont and what one can show in a photograph is still more frustrating. (It is worth remembering that the camera could not show the experience of railway travel either. Instead, it showed the locomotive-drawn train standing on its tracks in a still landscape.[3])

Is the last word that the camera can show the older city reasonably well but is less and less responsive to the newer city where the automobile has changed the order of things? And if the camera can show even the old parts so partially and approximately, can photographs possibly say anything about the essence of a city? To me there are two striking things about modern Cleveland. One is that it almost totally lacks what, as I was growing up in Boston, I though of as "city." To me the essence of "city" was streets lined with the fronts of single-family houses forming continuous brick walls. In Boston, across the Common from my neighborhood, there were of course department stores, office buildings, etc., but even they stood where previously there had been single-family houses. When I moved to New York, I found that where older single-family houses did not still wall the streets apartment houses, large and small, did so. New York City might be where one worked, but first of all it was where one wanted to live (all the while complaining). In place of this dense, desirable city, Cleveland has suburbs.

Clevelanders are of course not alone in opting for suburbs. James F. O'Gorman (himself from St. Louis, another city with no "city") writes that "by the 1880s American Society had begun to achieve that split personality, that division into commercial centers and domestic suburbs, toward which it had tended since early in the century and that would mark it for the coming century at least. . . . This backdrop of city and suburb . . . is the framework for the maturation of those two especially American building

3. See *The Railroad in American Art: Representations of Technological Change,* Susan Danly and Leo Marx, eds. (Cambridge, Mass.: MIT Press, 1988).

Photographs

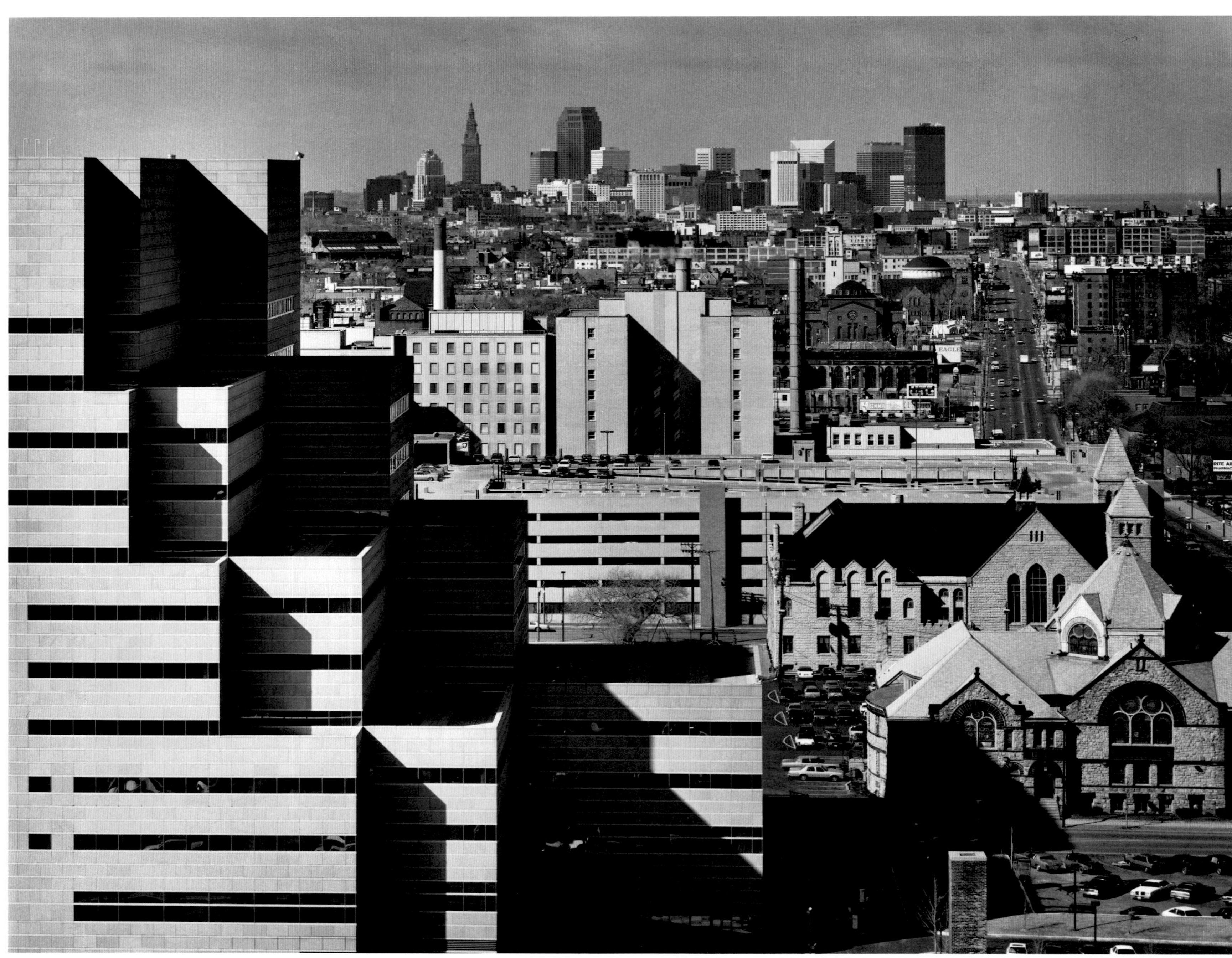

View of Downtown Looking Northwest. Left foreground: Outpatient Clinic, Cleveland Clinic. 1985. Cesar Pelli, architect. Right foreground: East Mount Zion Baptist Church (originally Euclid Avenue Christian Church). Ca. 1900. George Kramer, architect. March 1988.

U R B A N   V I R T U E

Indeed an abrupt transition is usually an urban virtue and one that photographs well.

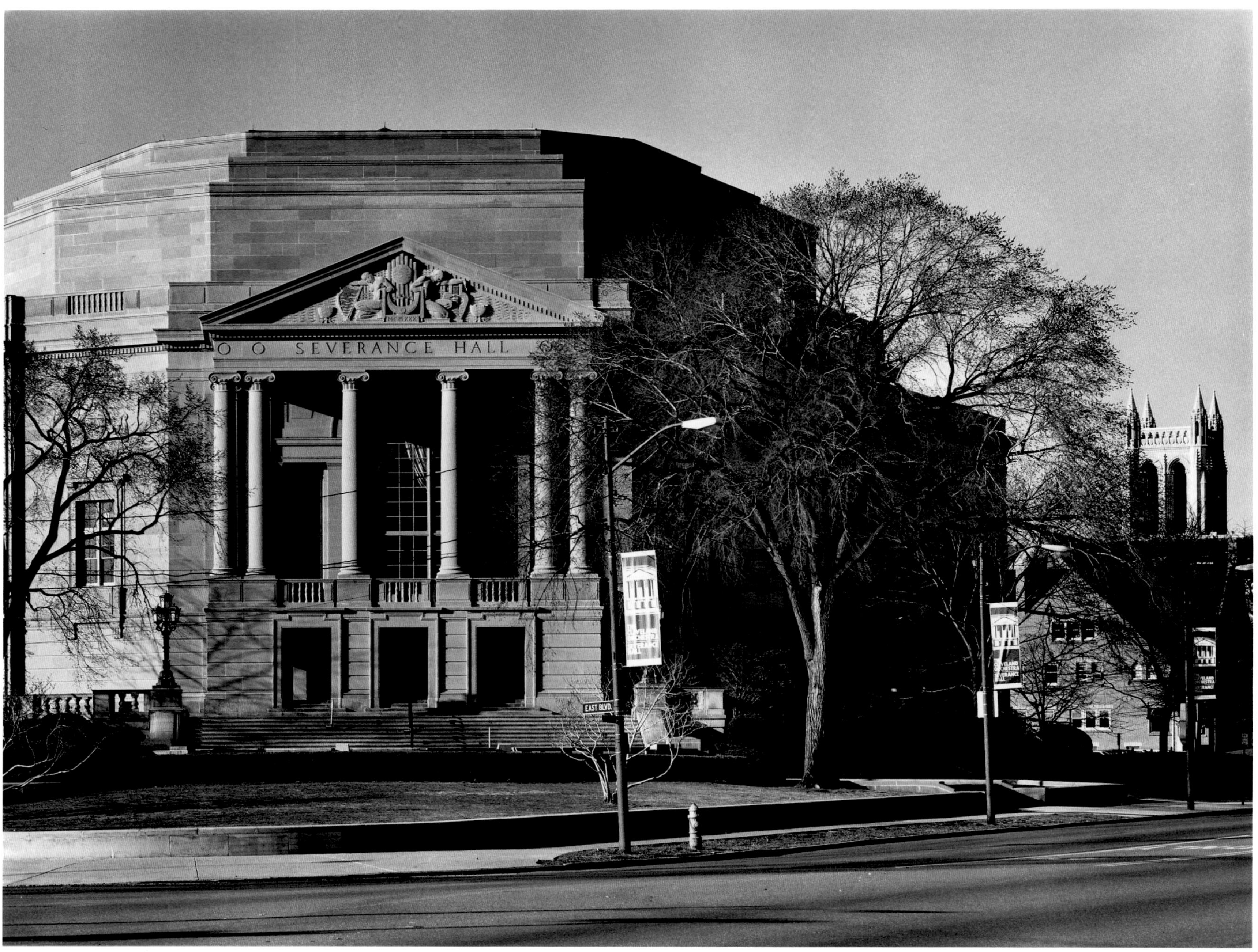

Severance Hall. 11001 Euclid Avenue. 1931. Walker and Weeks, architects. April 1989.

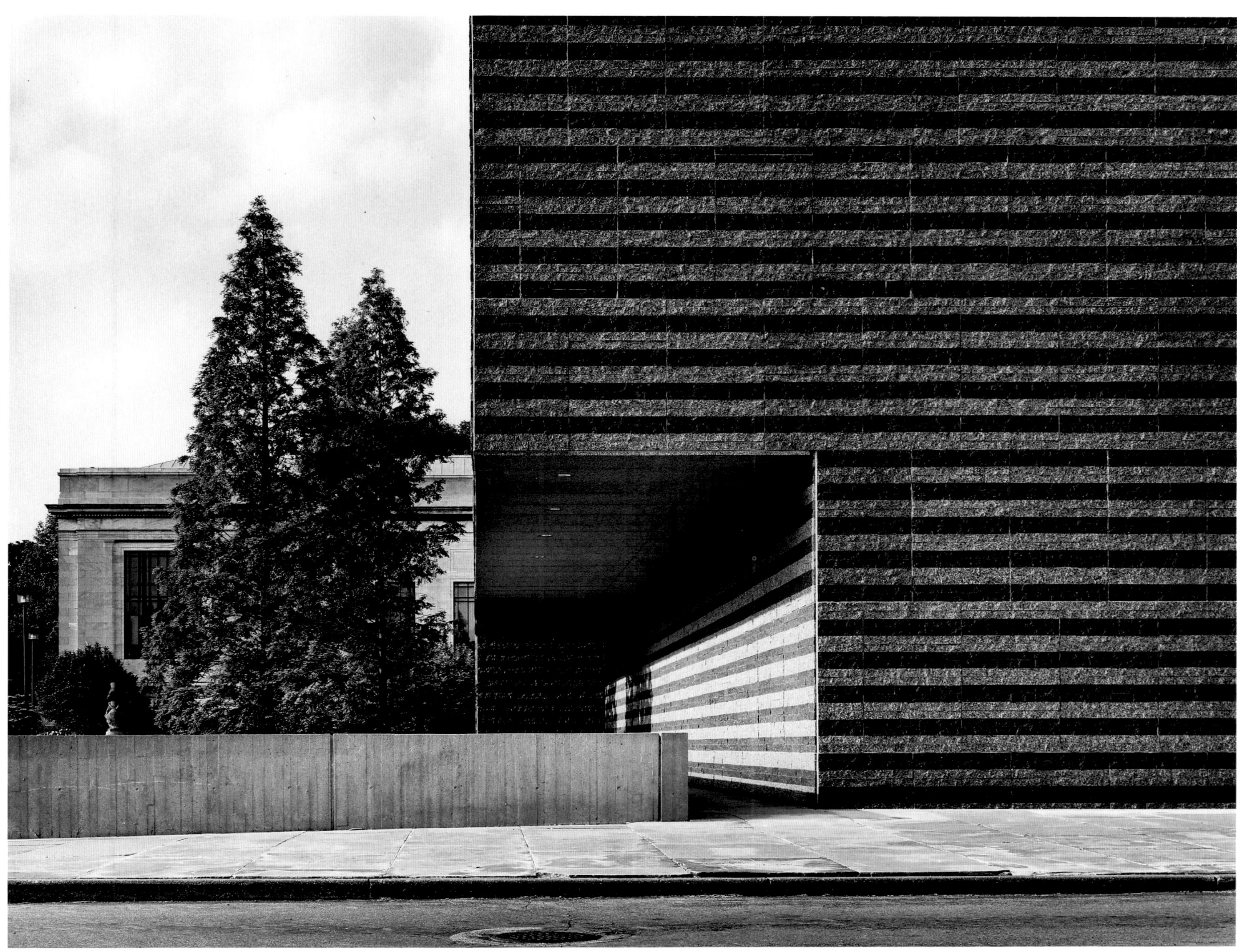

The Cleveland Museum of Art. 1916 Building: Hubbell and Benes, architects. 1970 Addition: Marcel Breuer and Hamilton P. Smith, architects. May 1988.

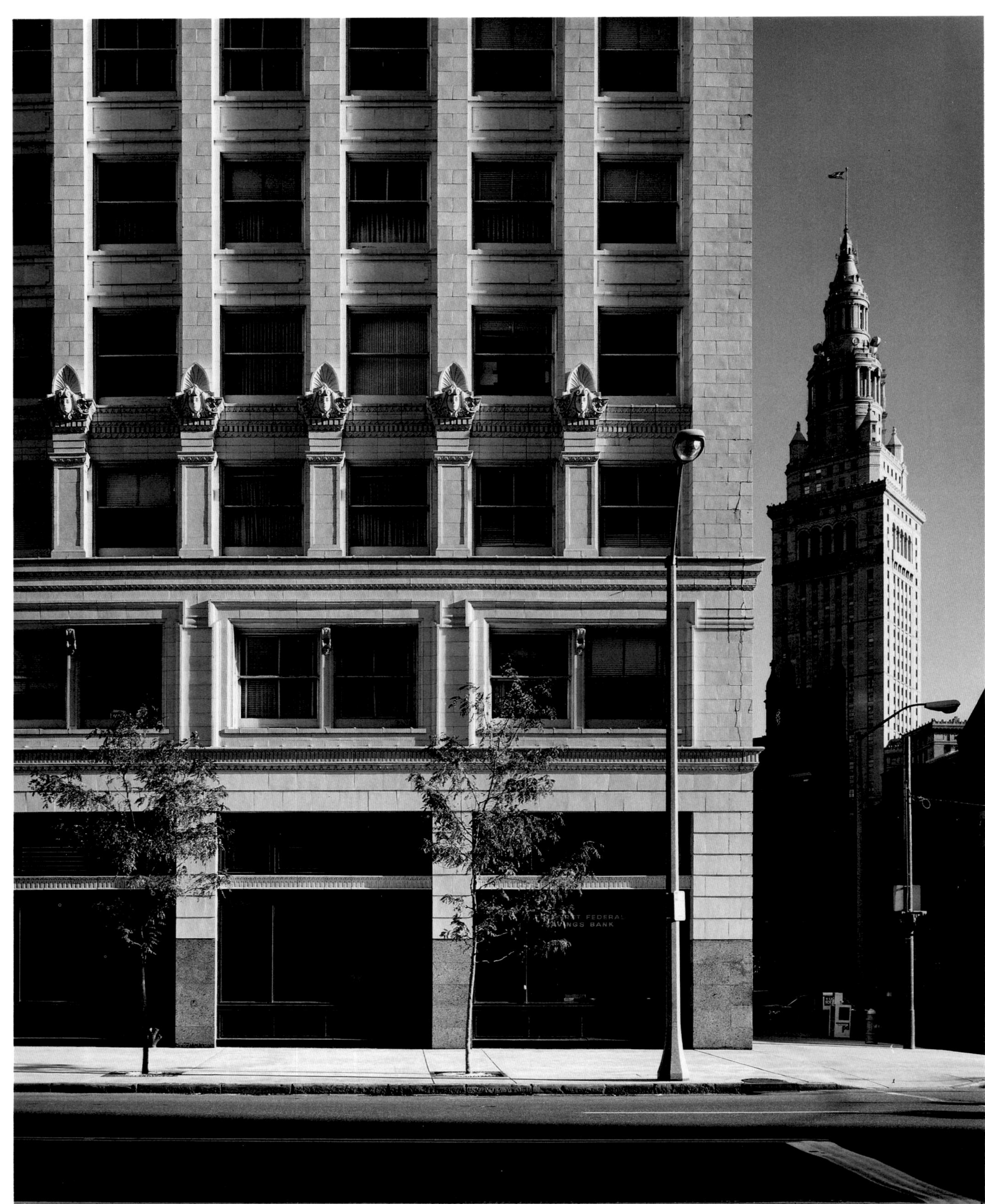

The Engineers Building (originally The Brotherhood of Locomotive Engineers Building, now demolished). 1914. Knox and Elliot, architects. October 1987

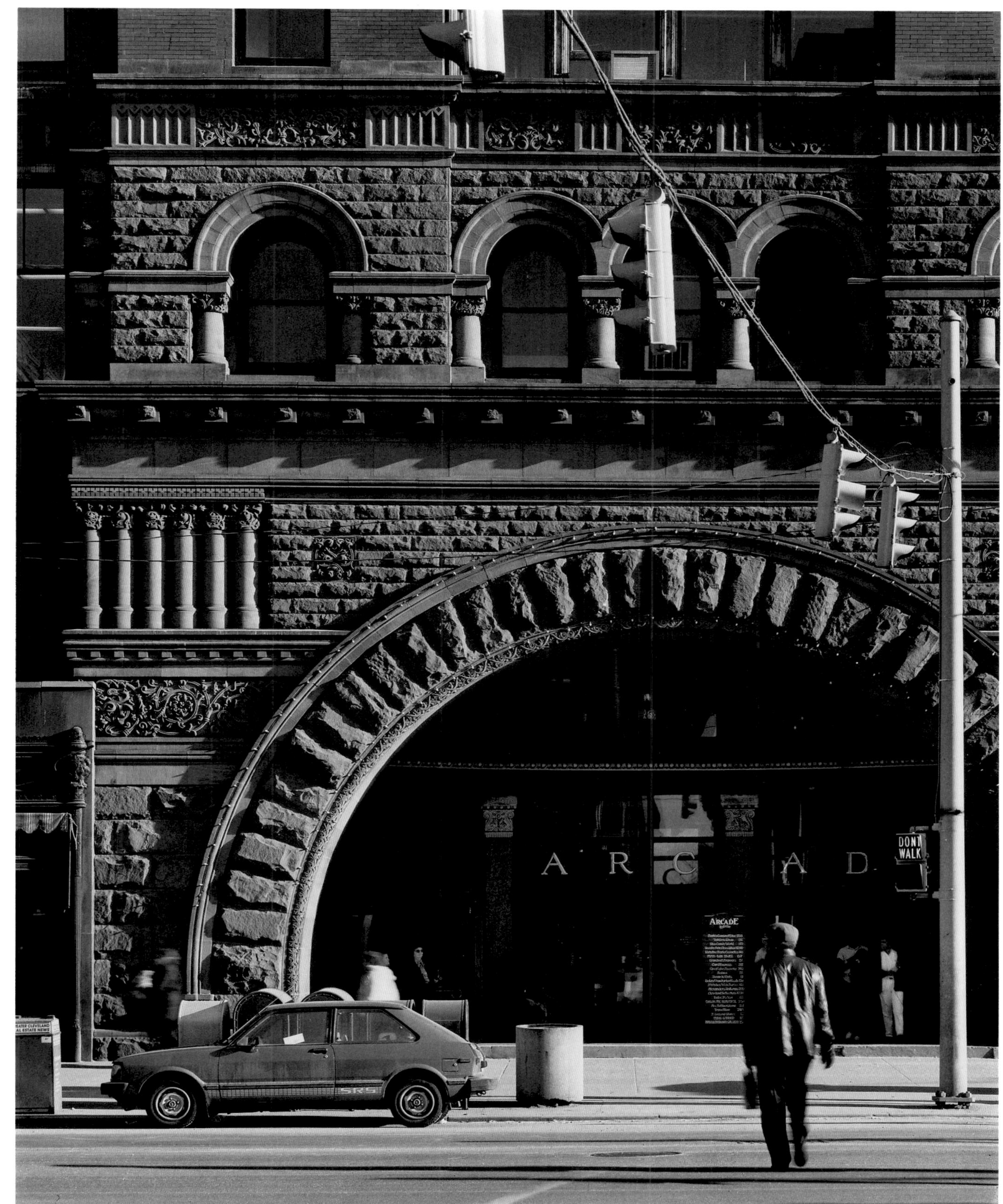

The Arcade, Superior Avenue Entrance. 401 Euclid Avenue. 1890. John Eisenmann and George H. Smith, architects. March 1988.

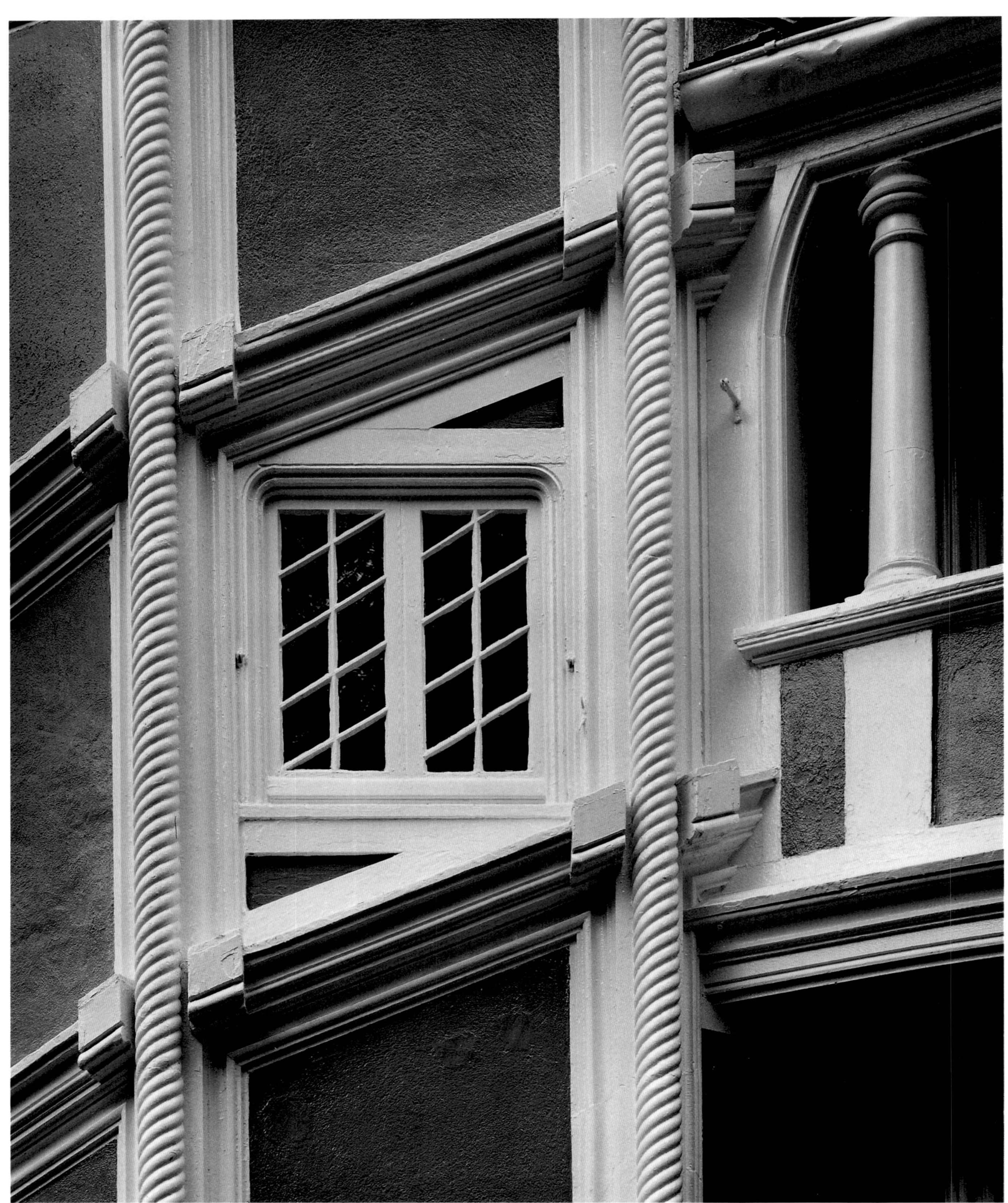

Turret Window, William H. Warner House. 2689 East Overlook Road, Cleveland Heights. 1908. Meade and Garfield, architects. October 1987.

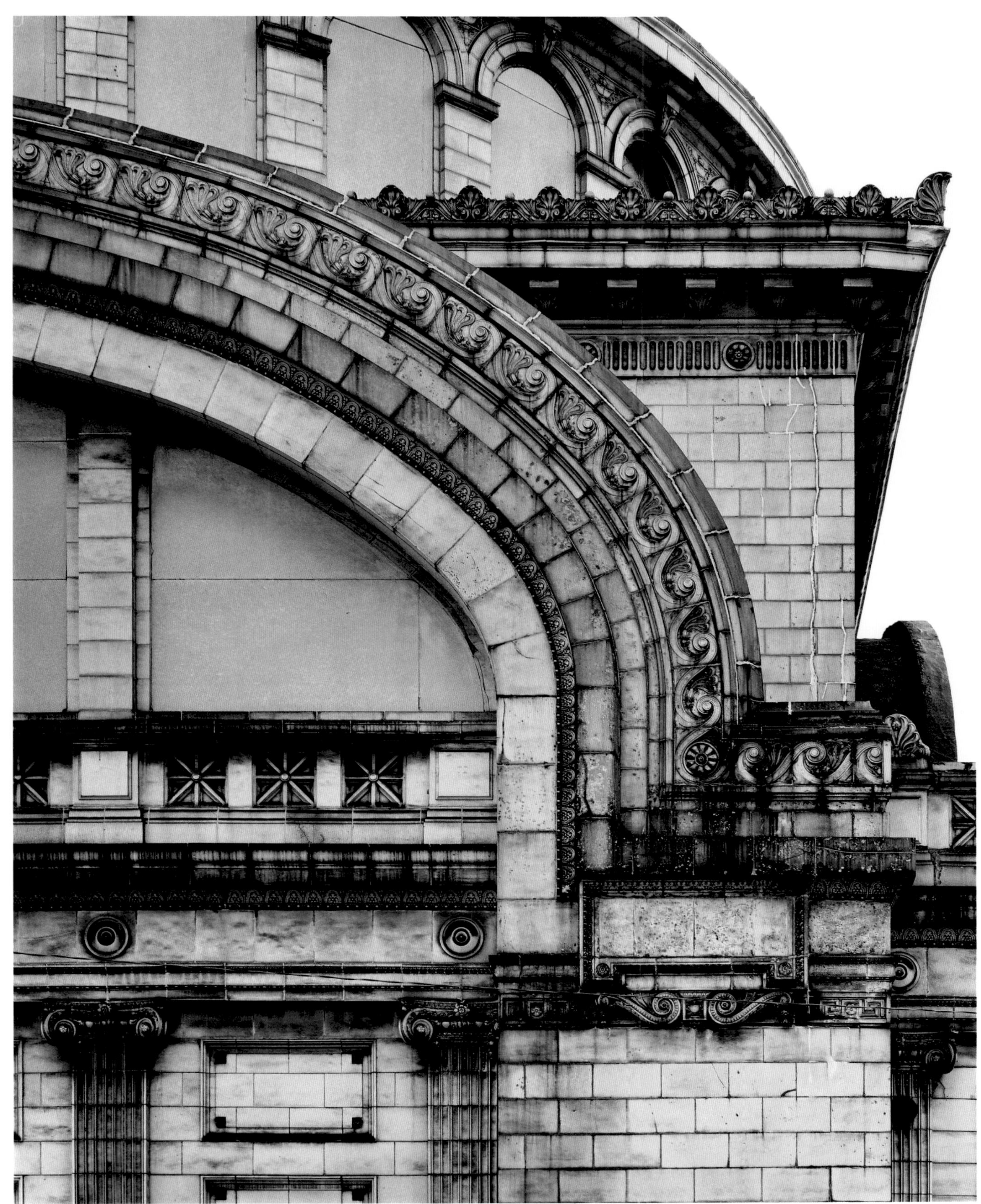

Church of God and True Holiness (originally Second Church of Christ, Scientist; later The Cleveland Playhouse). 7710 Euclid Avenue. 1916. Frederic Striebinger, architect. August 1987.

The camera's head-on perspective so resembles the architect's elevation that its response is simple and appropriate.

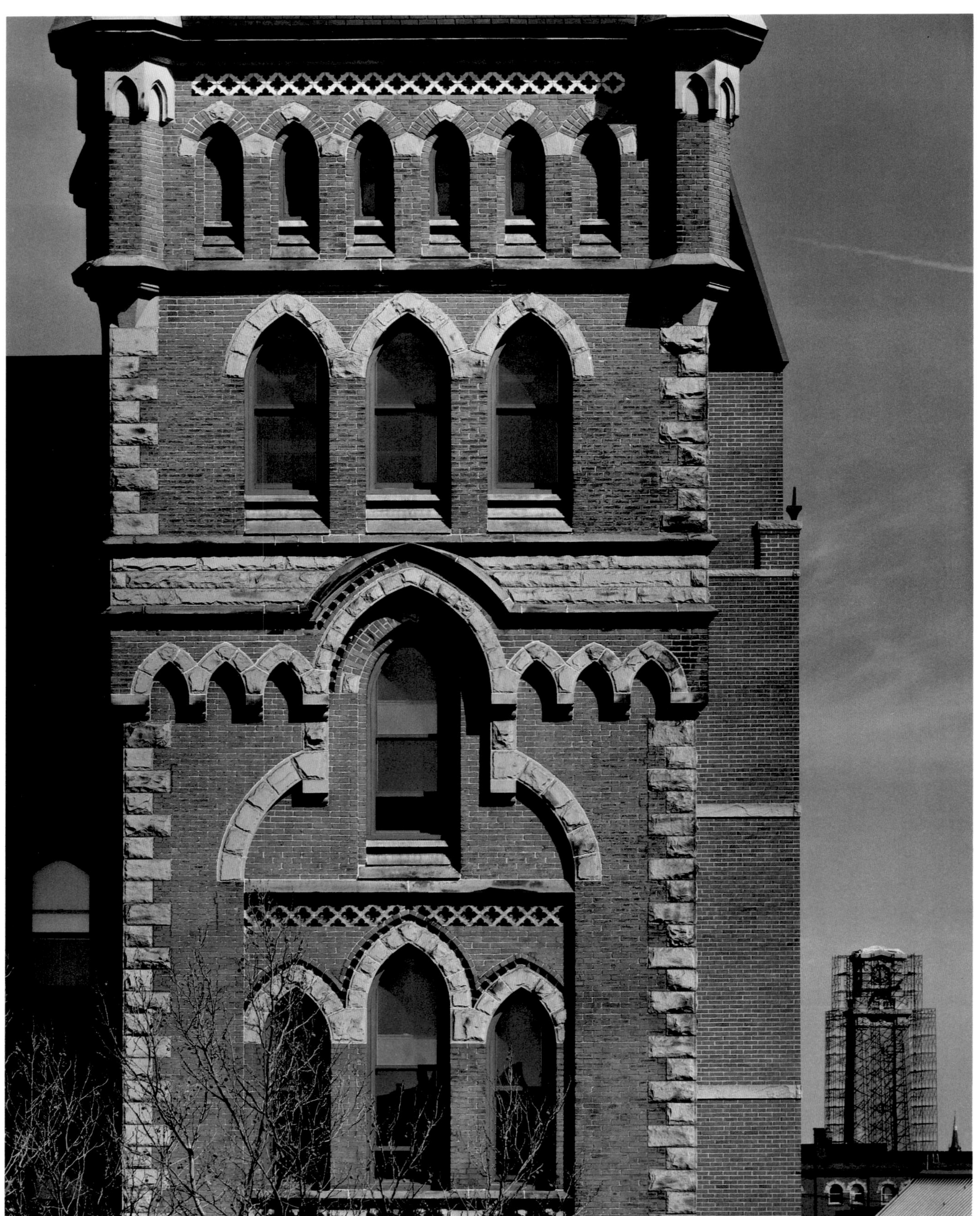

St. Ignatius High School (originally St. Ignatius College). 1911 West 30th Street. 1888-91. Architect probably Brother Wipfler, Society of Jesus. March 1988.

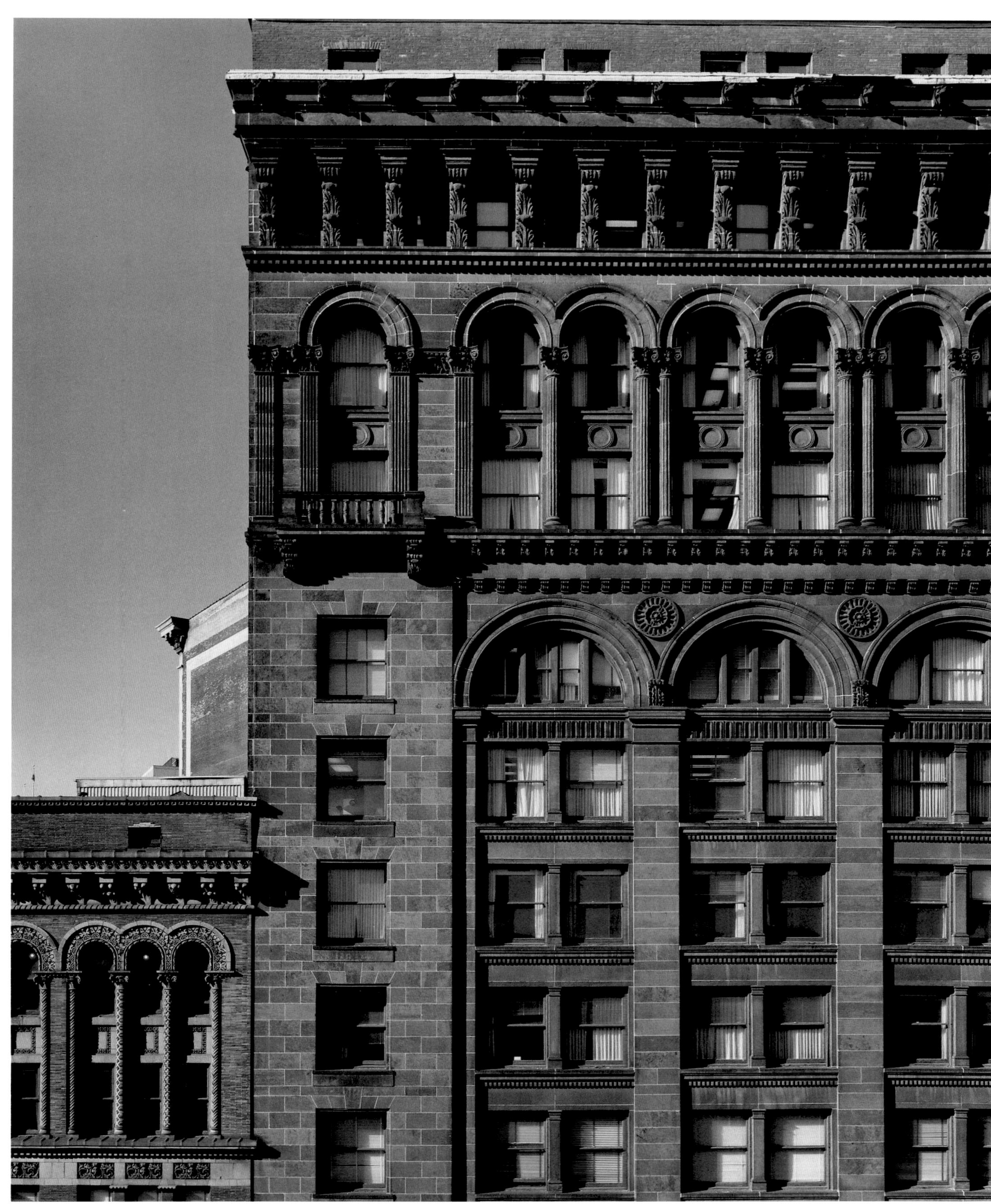

Old National City Bank Building (originally New England Building, later Guardian Bank Building). 623 Euclid Avenue. 1896. Shepley, Rutan, and Coolidge, architects. Façade altered and main banking hall remodeled 1915. Walker and Weeks, architects. *Garfield Building* (left). Euclid Avenue and East 6th Street. 1893. Henry Ives Cobb, architect. March 1988.

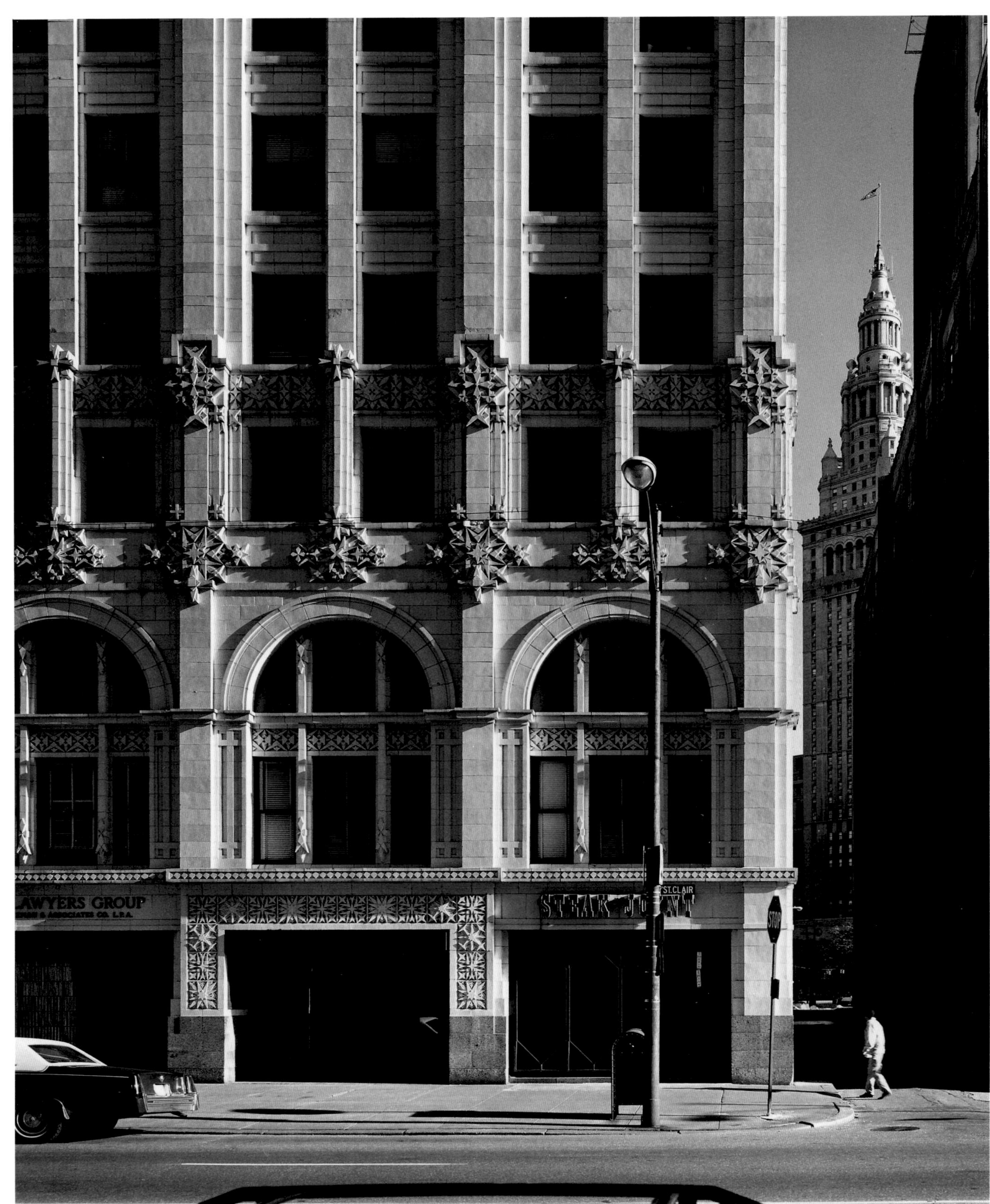

The Standard Building (originally the Engineers Bank Building). 1370 Ontario Street. 1924. Knox and Elliot, architects. October 1987.

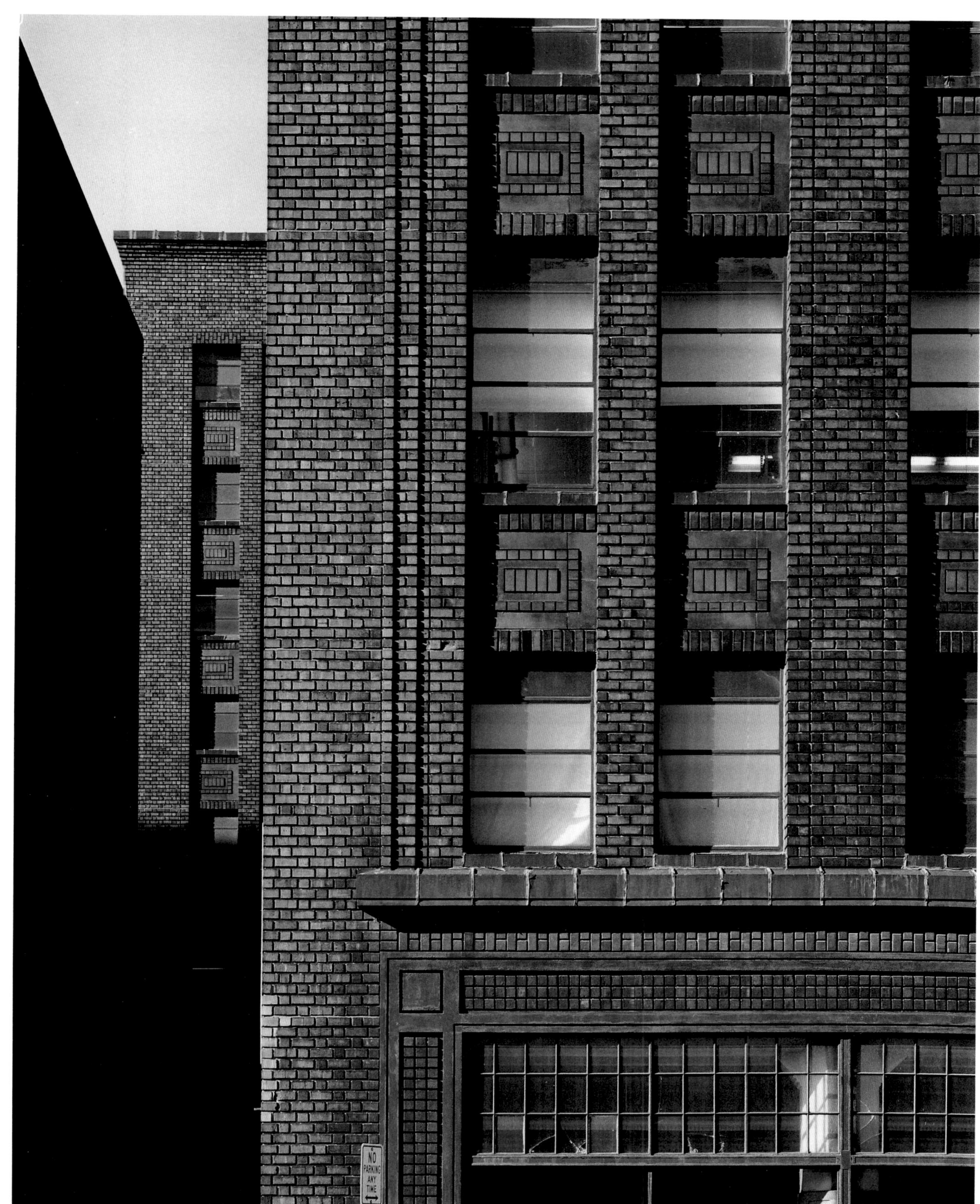

The Bingham Building (originally the Bingham Company Warehouse). 1278 West 9th Street. 1915. Walker and Weeks, architects. October 1987.

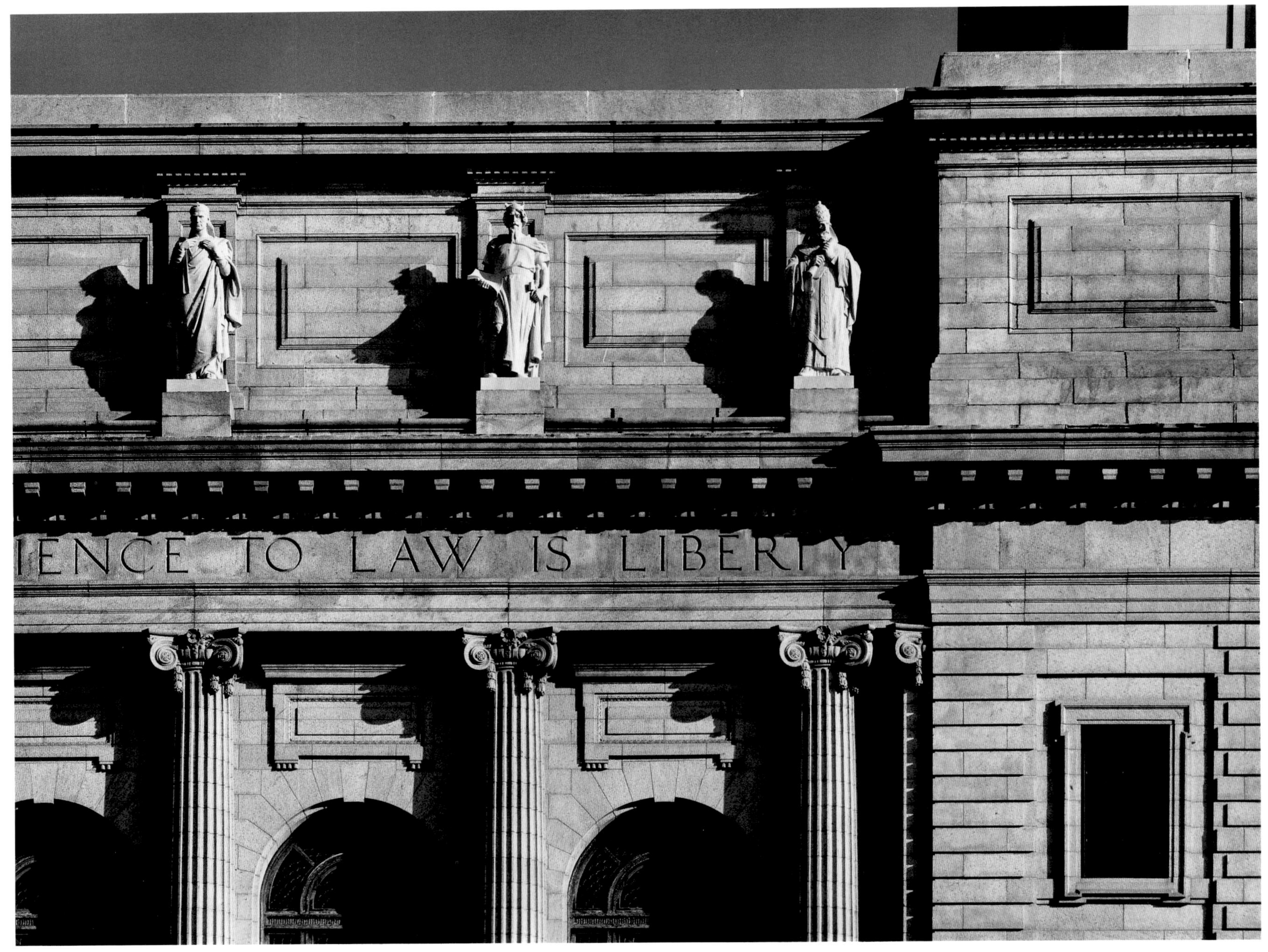

Sculptures on the North Façade of the Cuyahoga County Courthouse. 1 Lakeside Avenue NW. 1912. Lehman and Schmitt, architects. Charles Morris, designer. Herman Matzen and Isadore Konti, sculptors. April 1989.

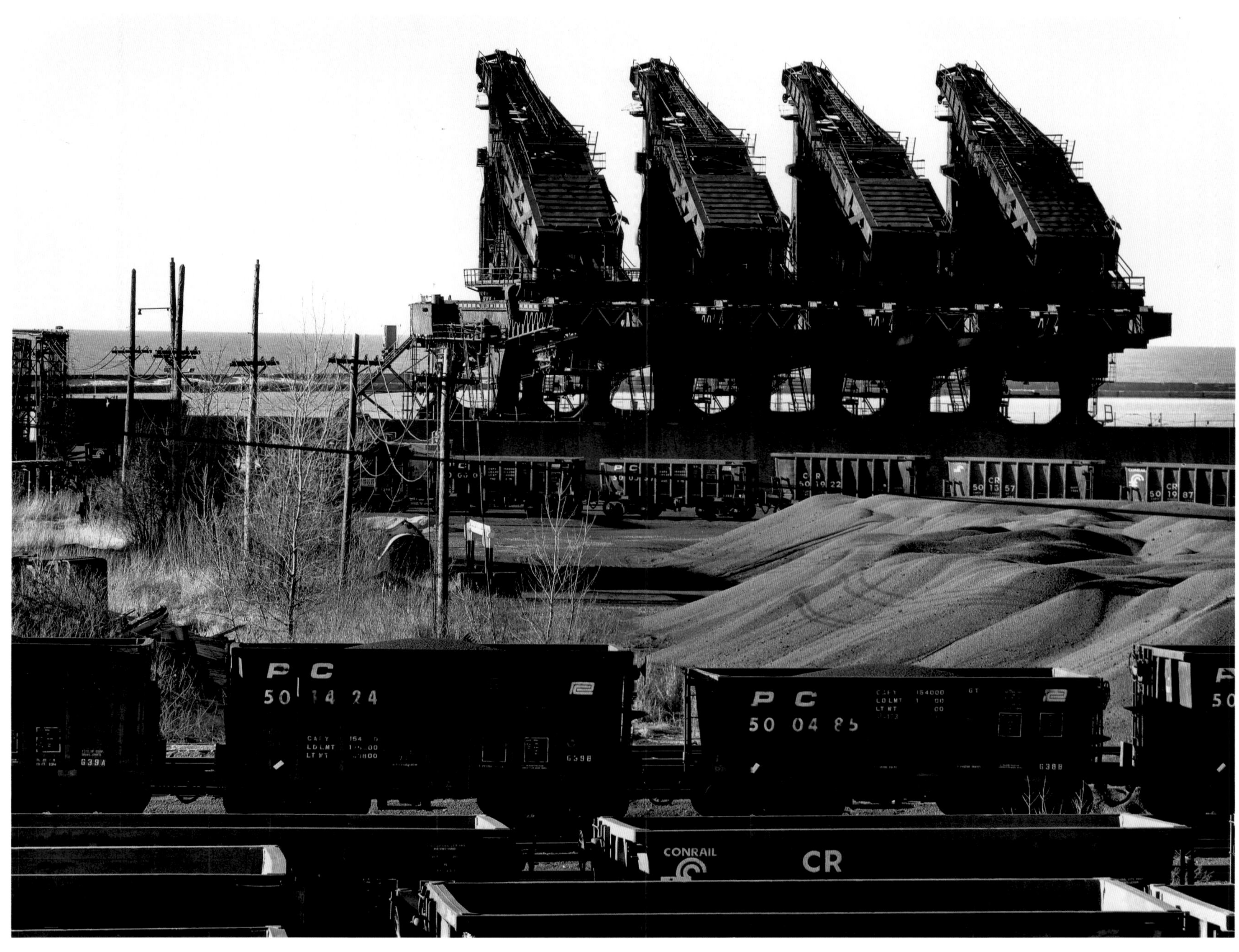

Hulett Unloaders ("Grasshoppers"), Whiskey Island. Installed 1912. March 1988.

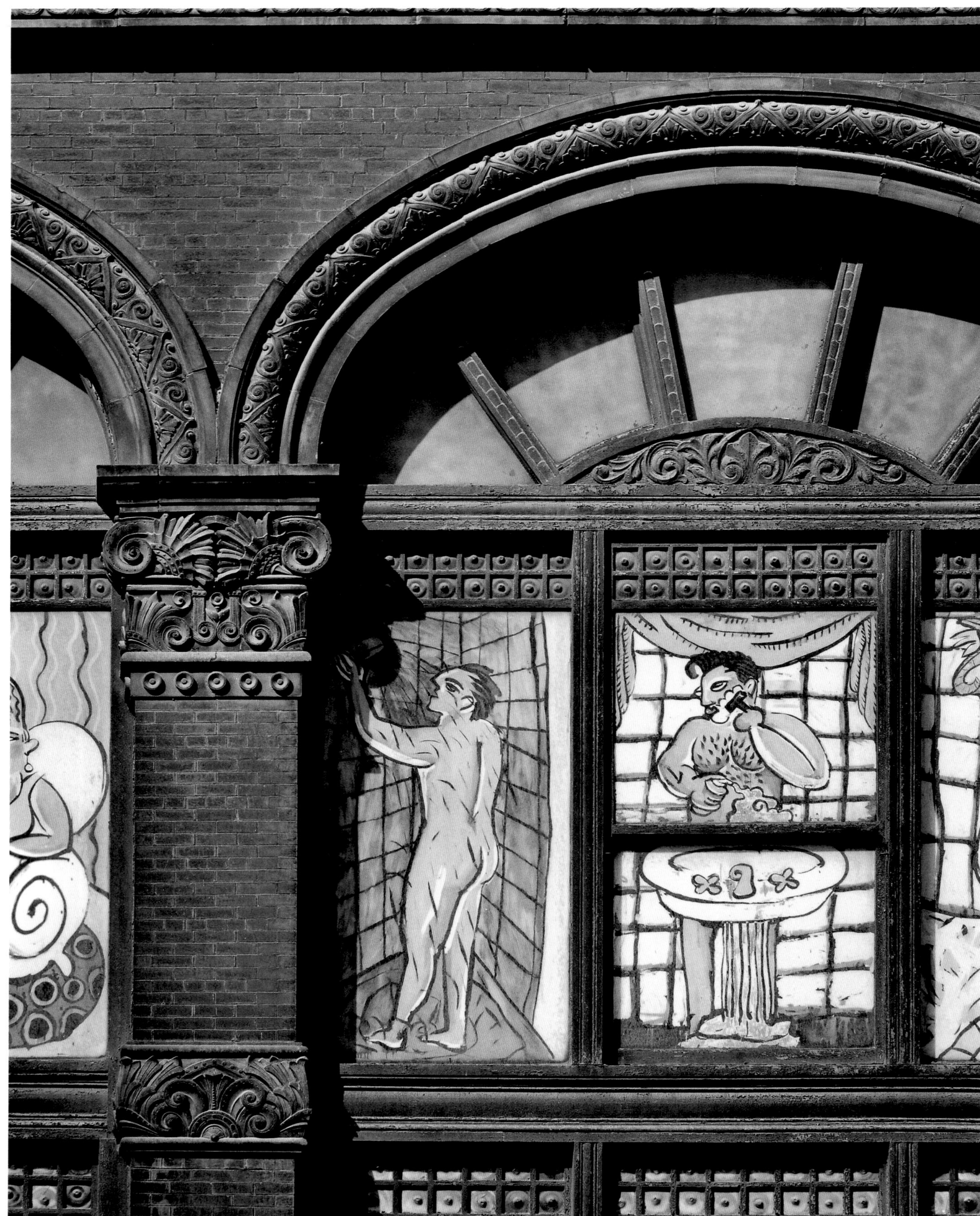

Detail of the Root and McBride Building with Scenes from "True Grit: The Great Lakes Citizen." 1220 West 6th Street. 1884. Cudell and Richardson, architects. Paintings completed 1986. George Bowes, Leslie Nichol, and Dan Postotnik, artists. May 1988.

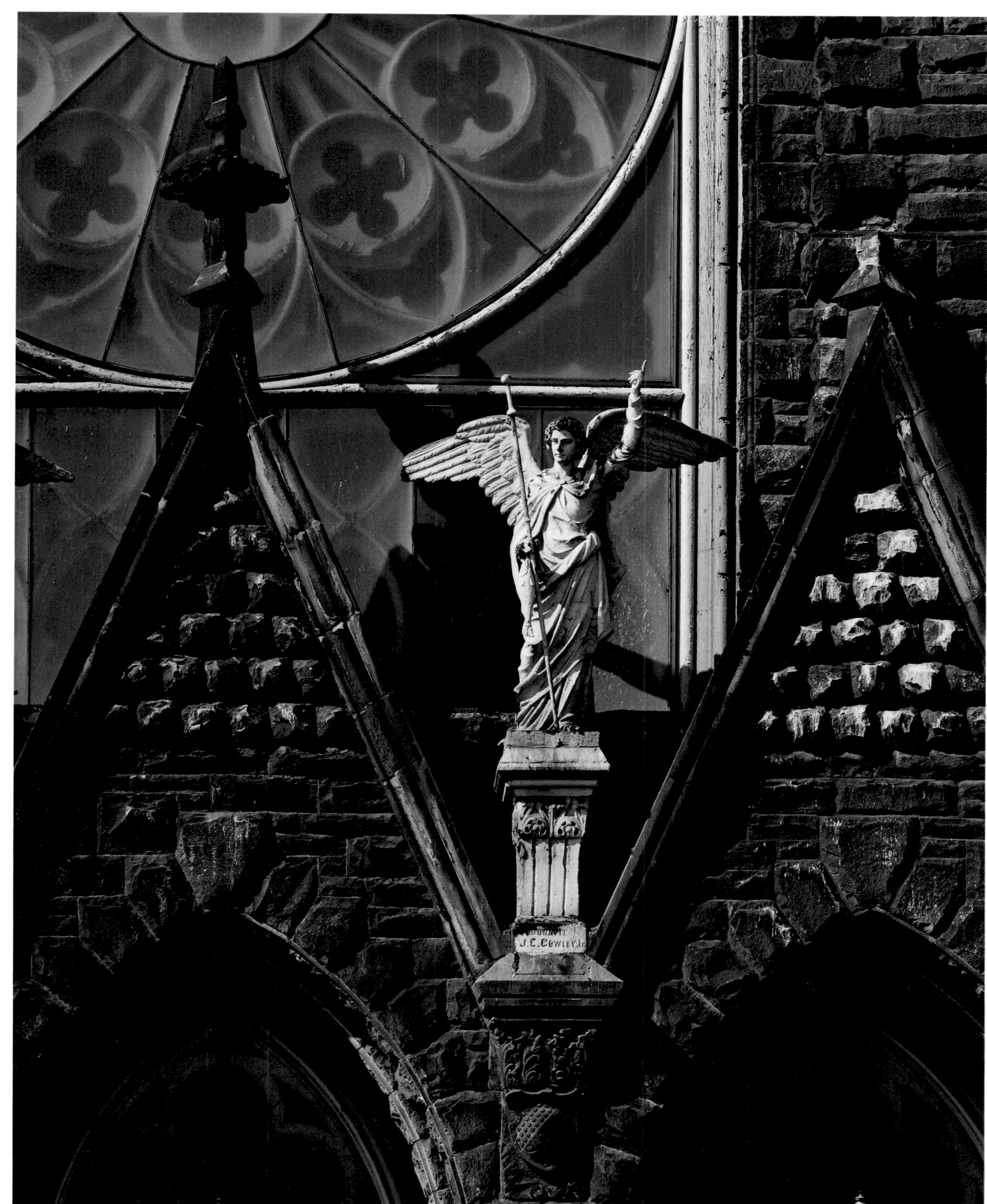

Archangel, St. Michael's Roman Catholic Church. 3114 Scranton Road. 1892. Adolph Druiding, architect. September 1987.

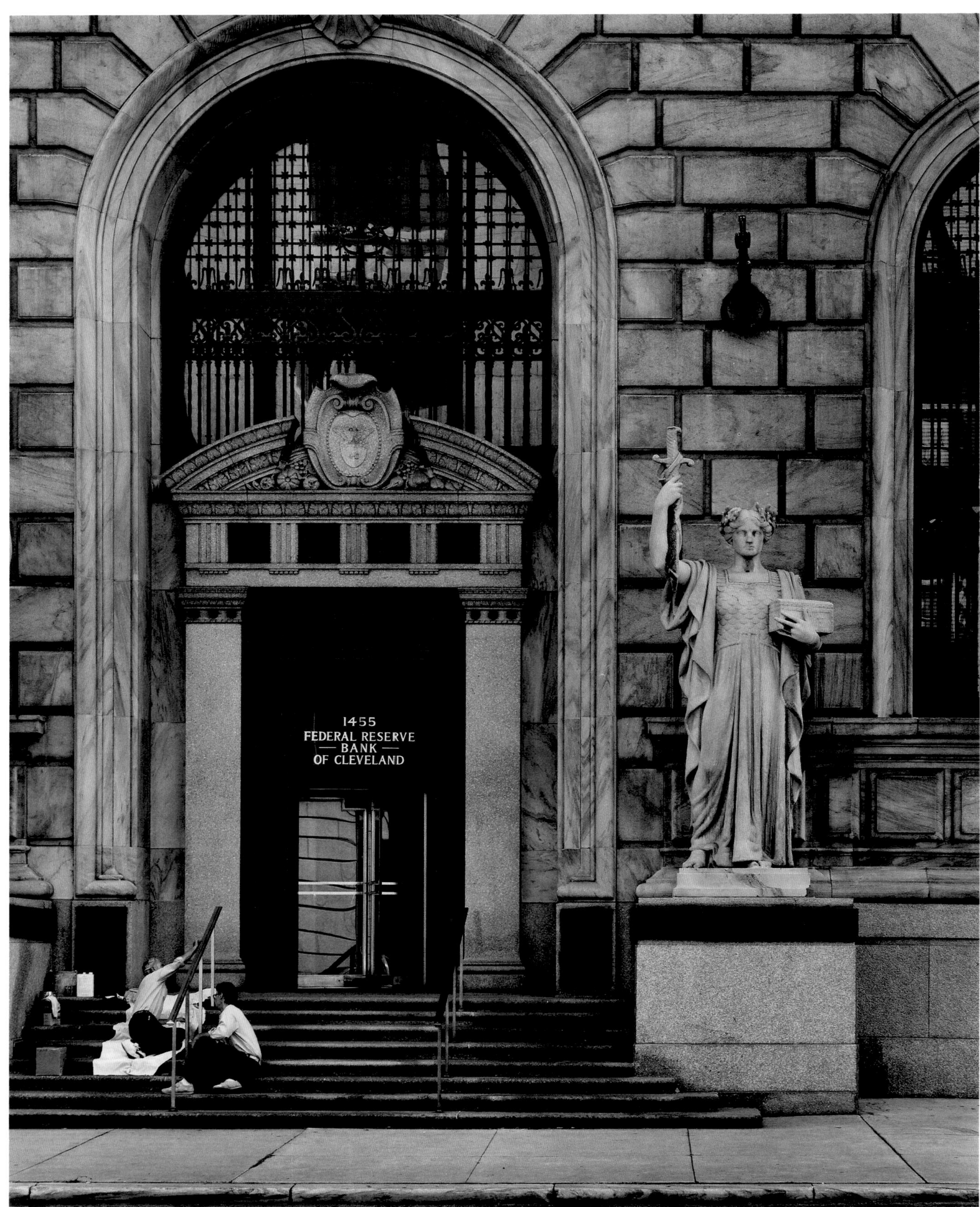

"Security," The Federal Reserve Bank. East 6th Street and Superior Avenue. 1923. Walker and Weeks, architects. Henry Hering, sculptor. July 1987.

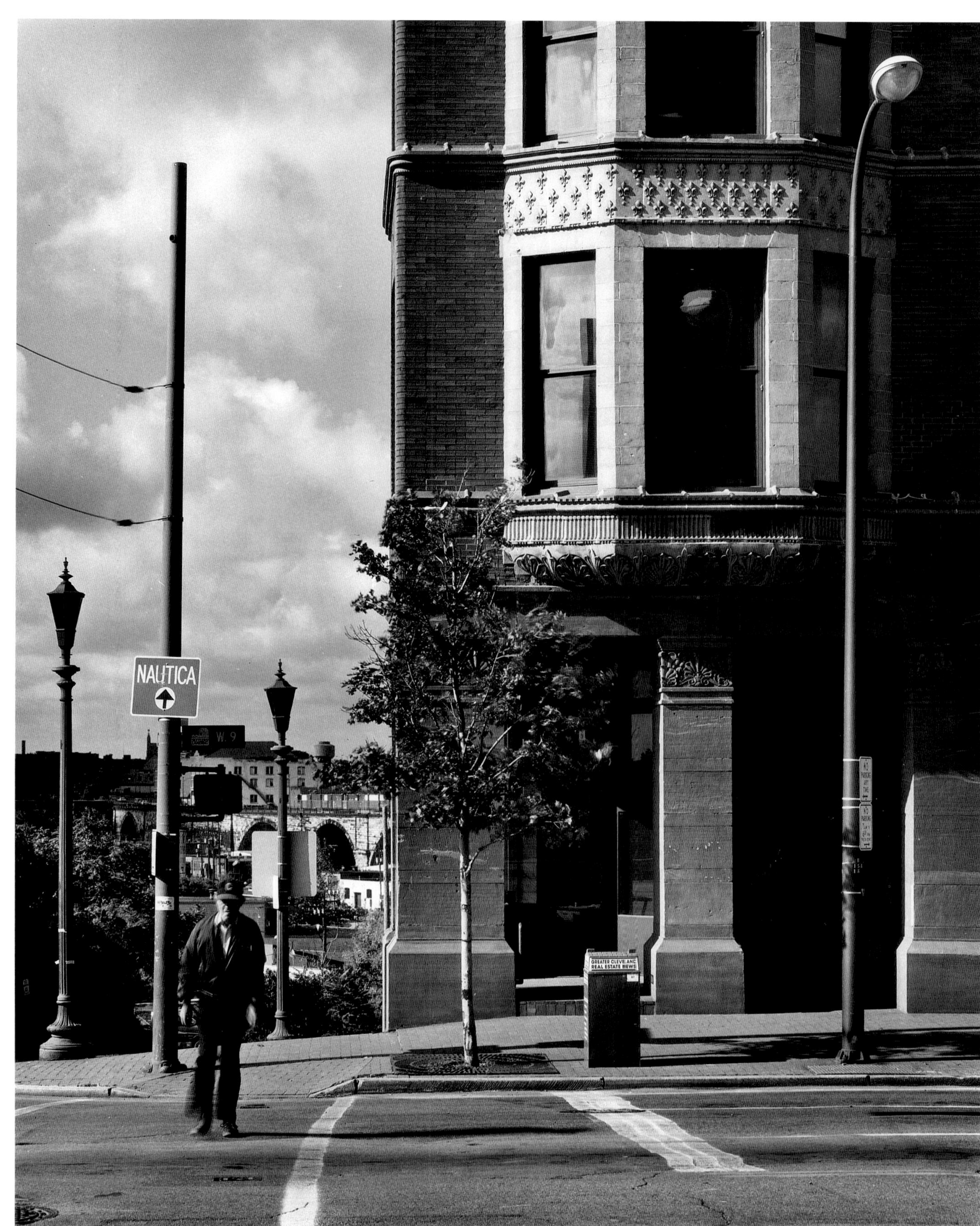

Western Reserve Building. West 9th Street and Superior Avenue. 1891. Burnham and Root, architects. September 1987.

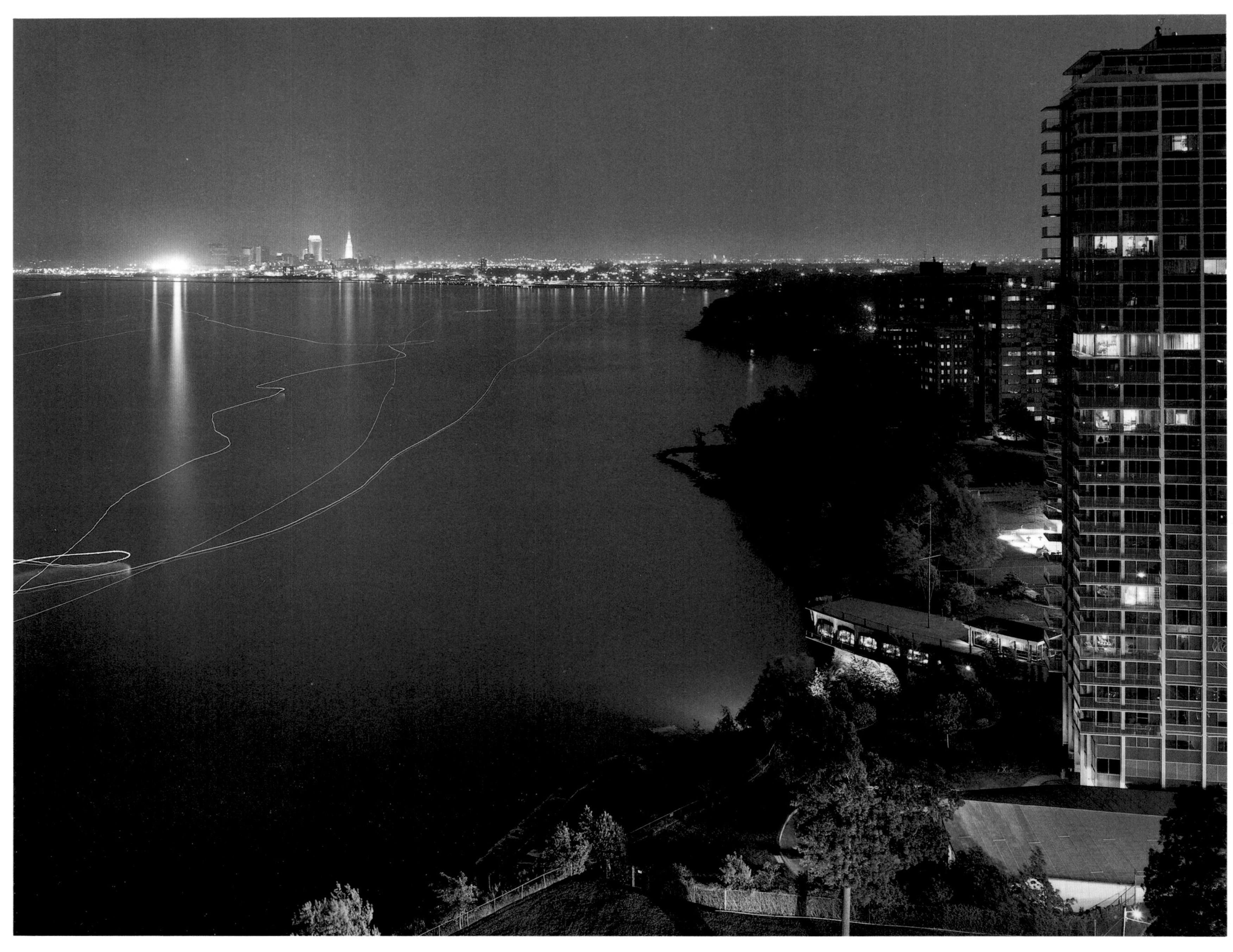

Night View of Cleveland's Coast-line. May 1988.

M O N O L O G U E S

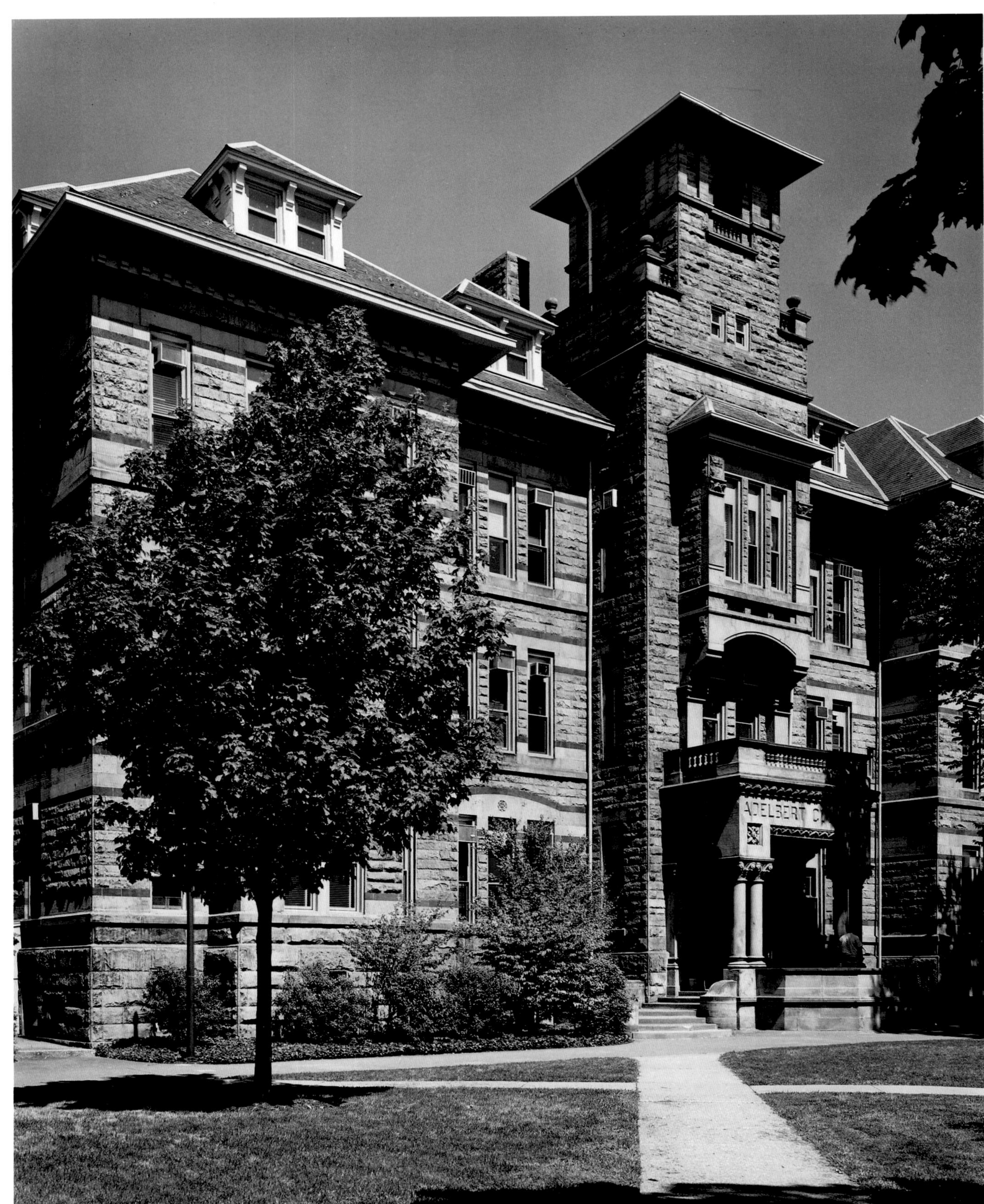

Adelbert Hall (originally Adelbert College, Western Reserve University). Case Western Reserve University. 1881-82. Joseph Ireland, architect. July 1988.

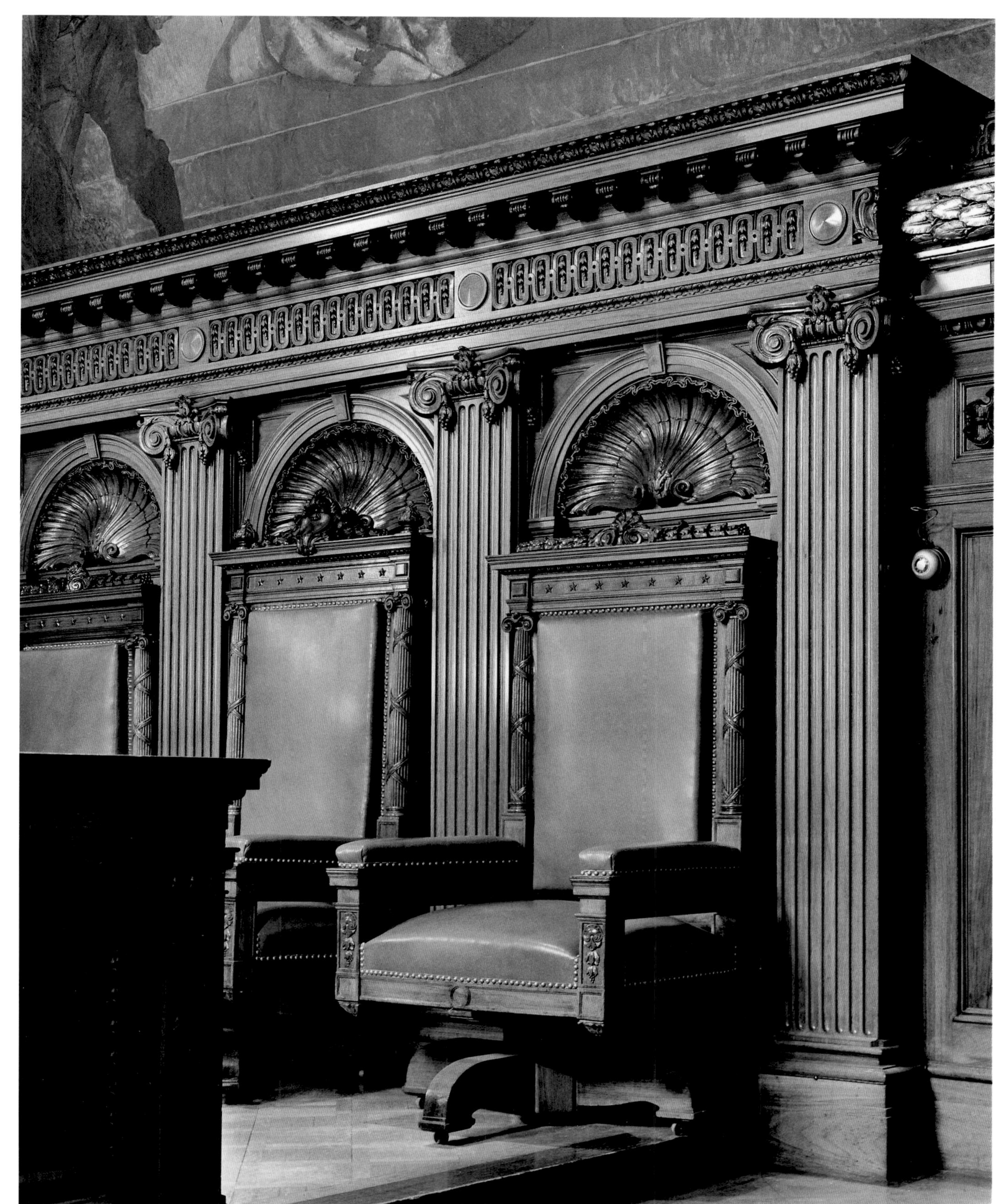

U. S. District Courtroom, The Federal Building (originally old U. S. Post Office, Custom House, and Court House). Superior Avenue at Public Square. 1910. Arnold W. Brunner, architect. February 1988.

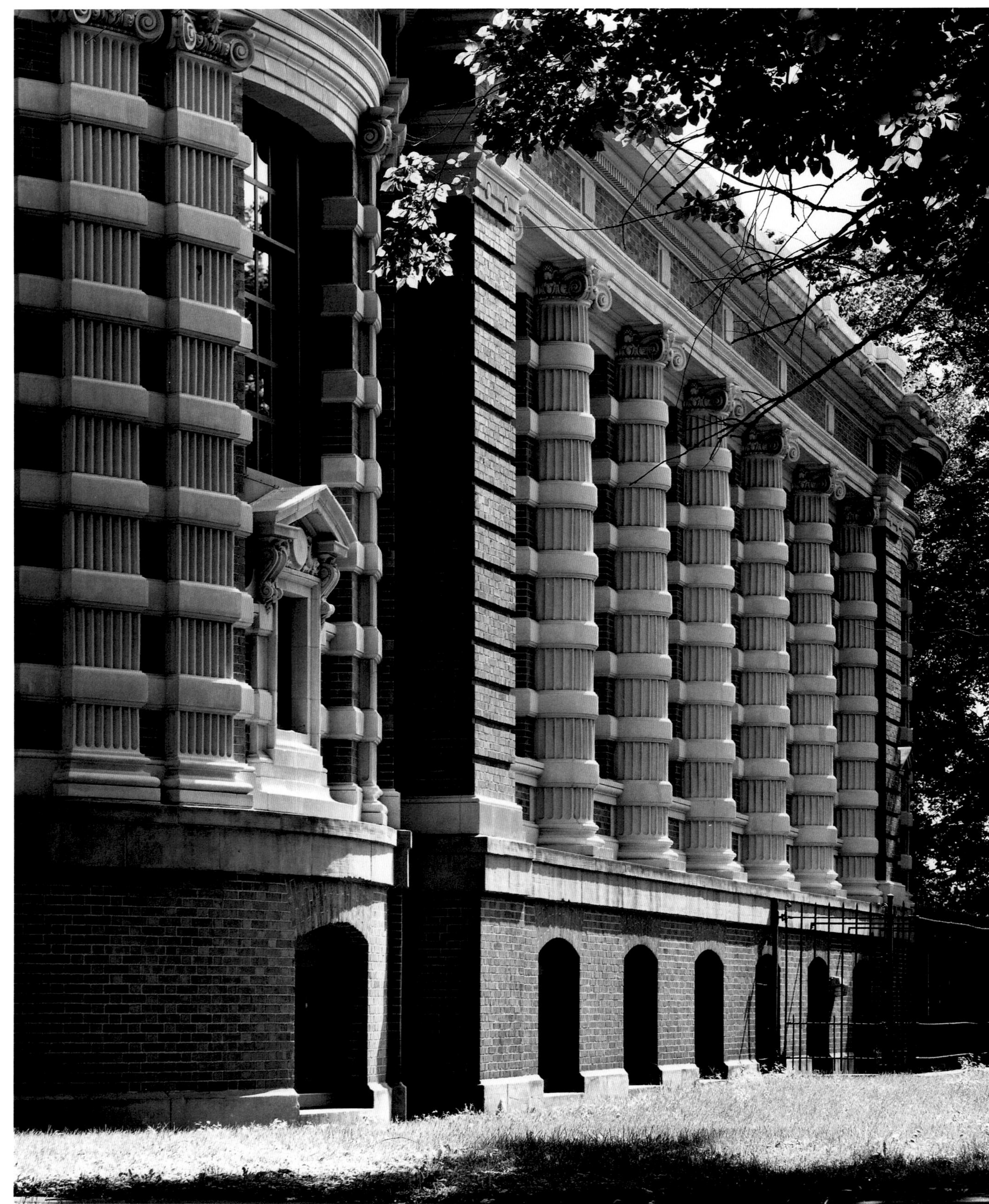

Carnegie West Library. 1900 Fulton Road. 1910. Edward L. Tilton, architect. October 1987.

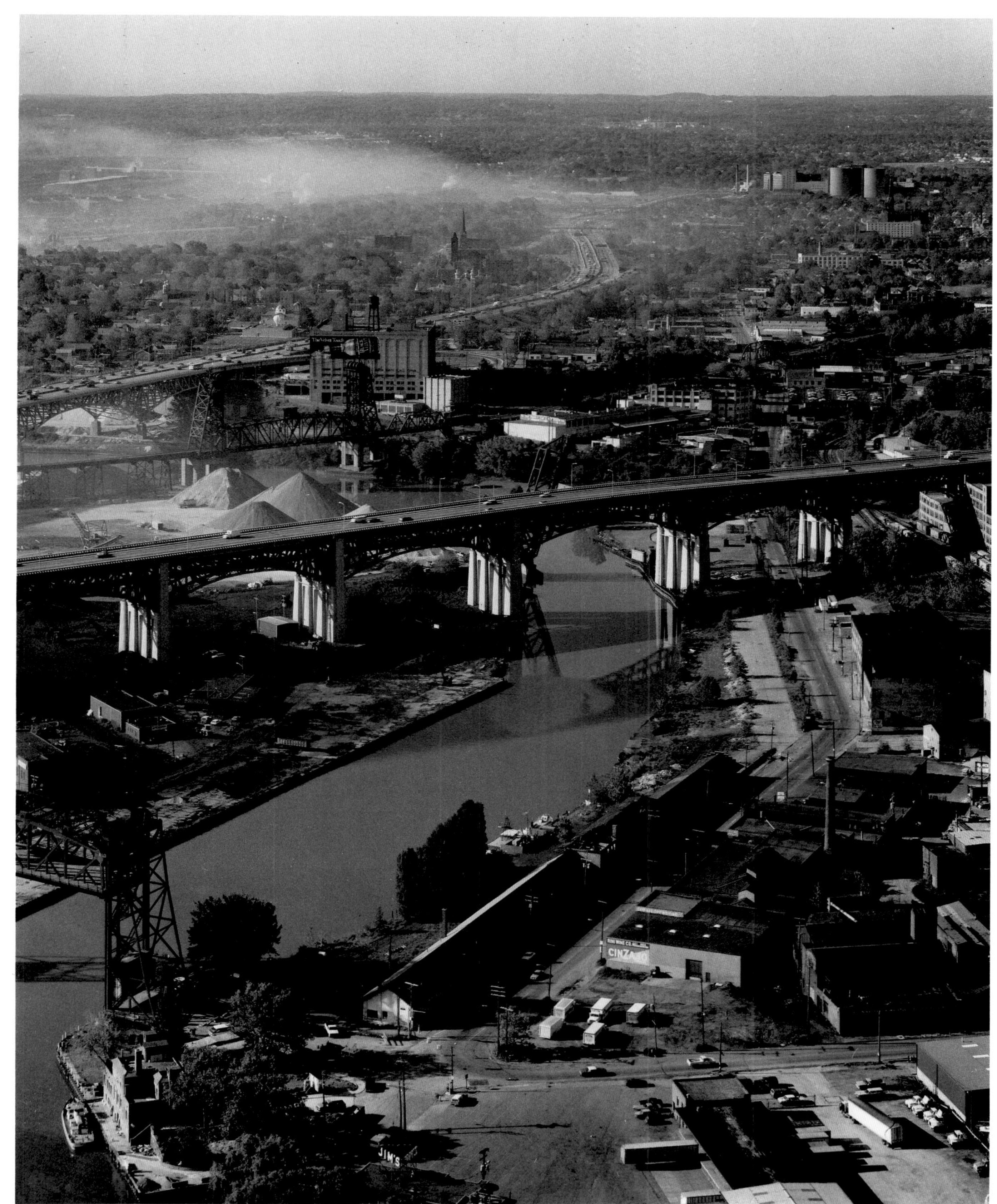

View Upriver from Terminal Tower Looking Toward Main Avenue Bridge. Bridge opened 1939. John O. McWilliams, county engineer. Wilbur J. Watson, consulting engineer. May 1988.

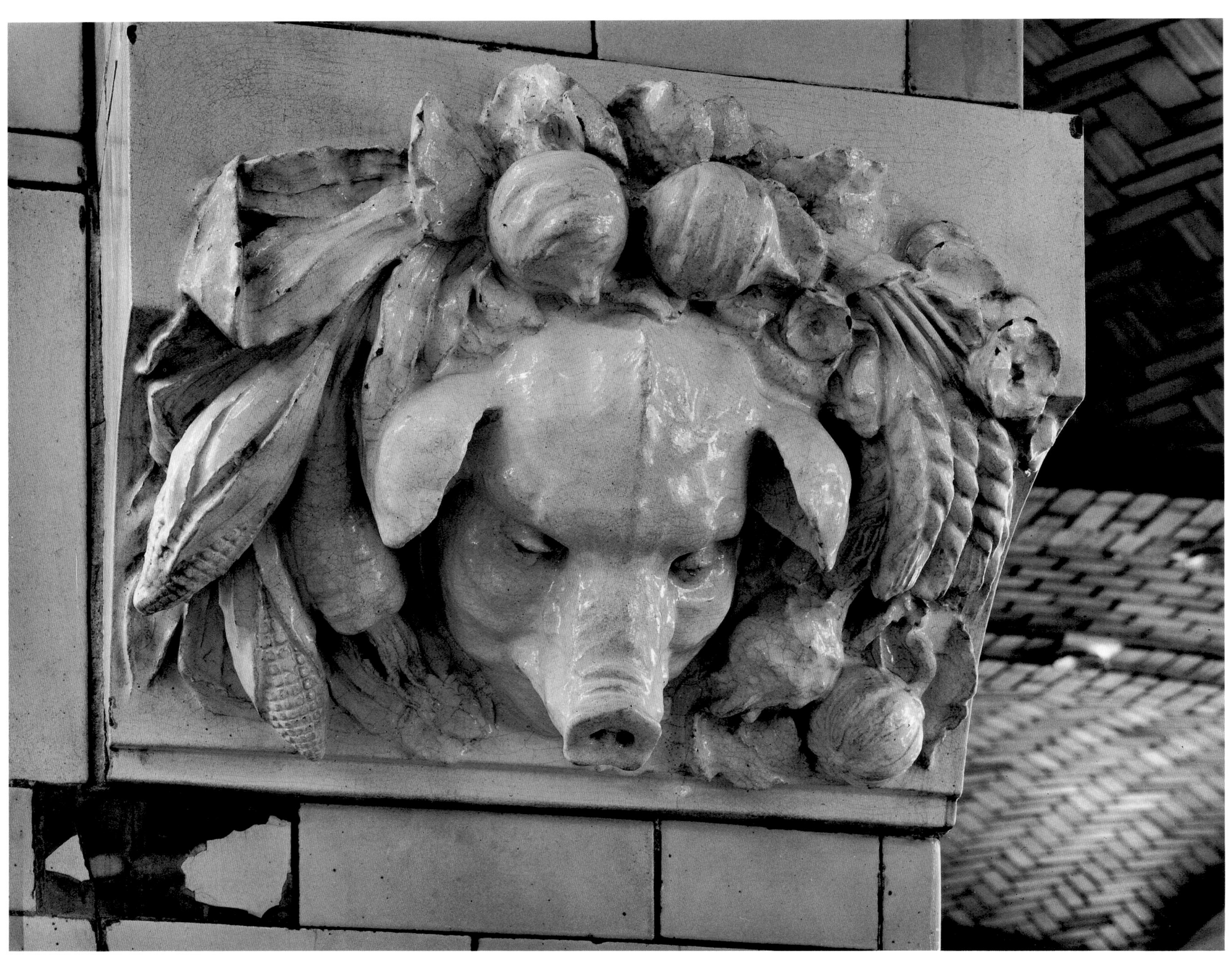

Capital, West Side Market. West 25th Street and Lorain Avenue. 1912. Hubbell and Benes, architects. February 1988.

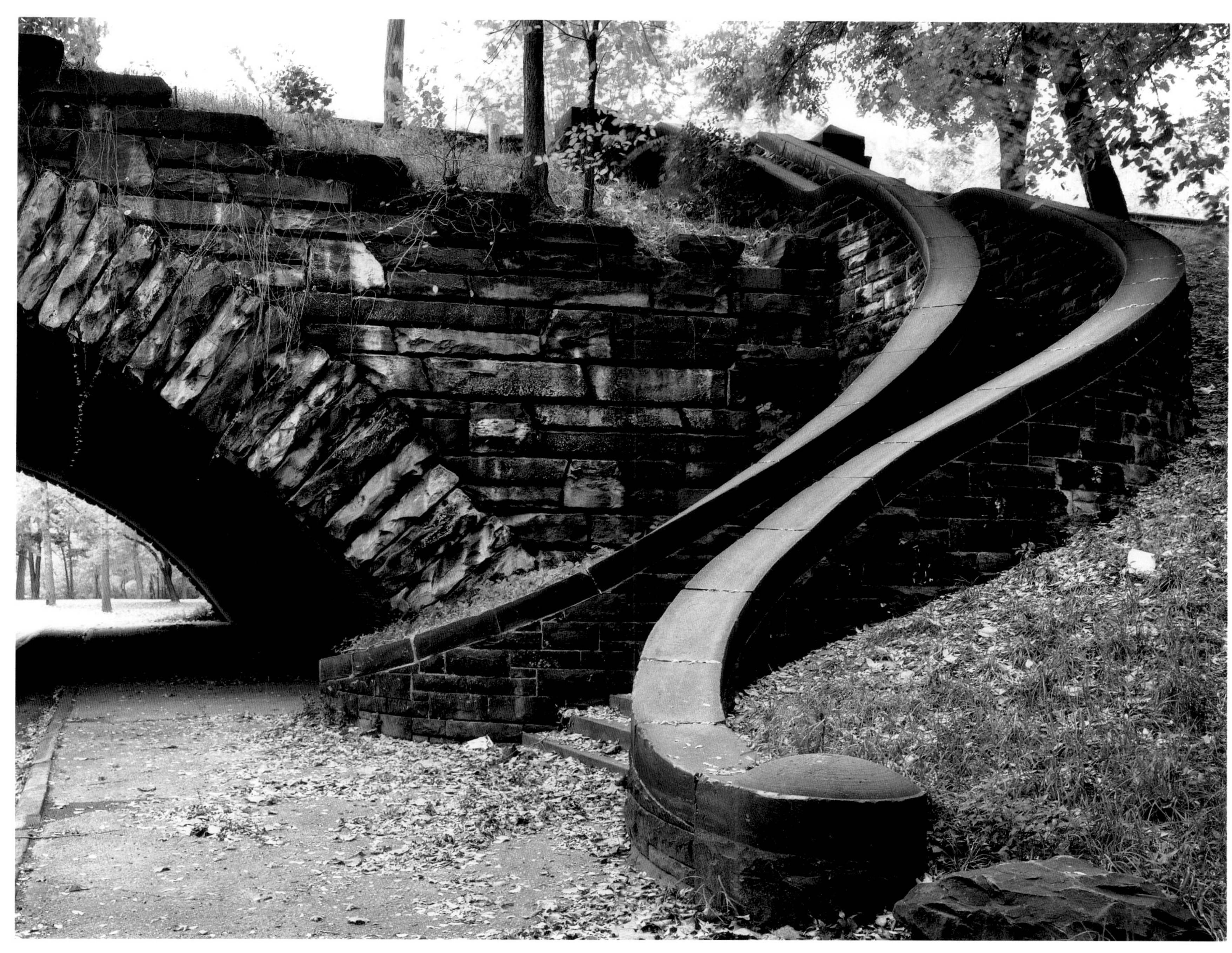

Wade Park Avenue Bridge. Rockefeller Park. 1899. Charles F. Schweinfurth, architect. October 1987.

Like any traveller I want a city to be different, even exotic.

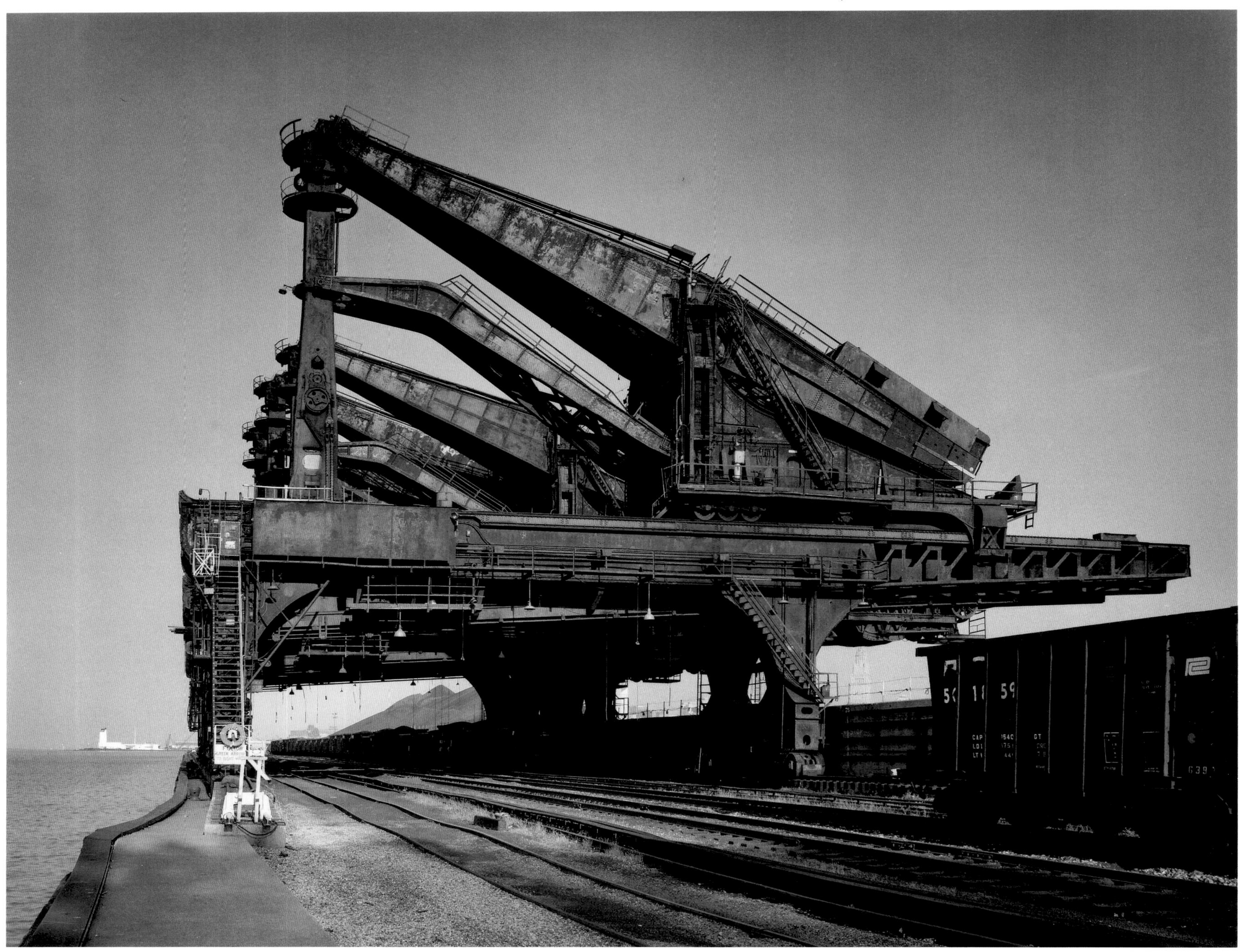

Hulett Unloaders (''Grasshoppers''). Whiskey Island. Installed 1912. October 1987.

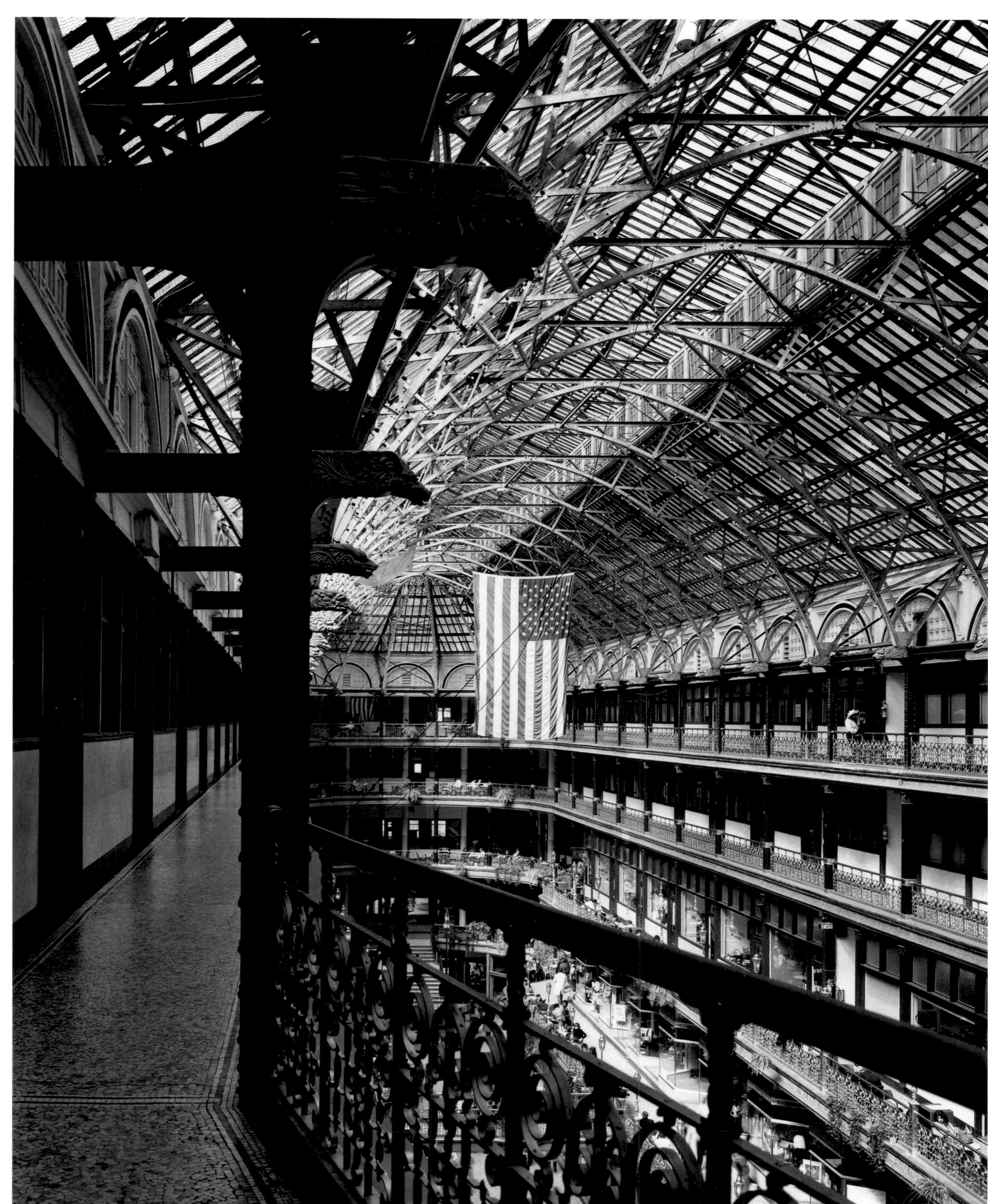

Interior, The Arcade. 401 Euclid Avenue. 1890. John Eisenmann and George H. Smith, architects. March 1988.

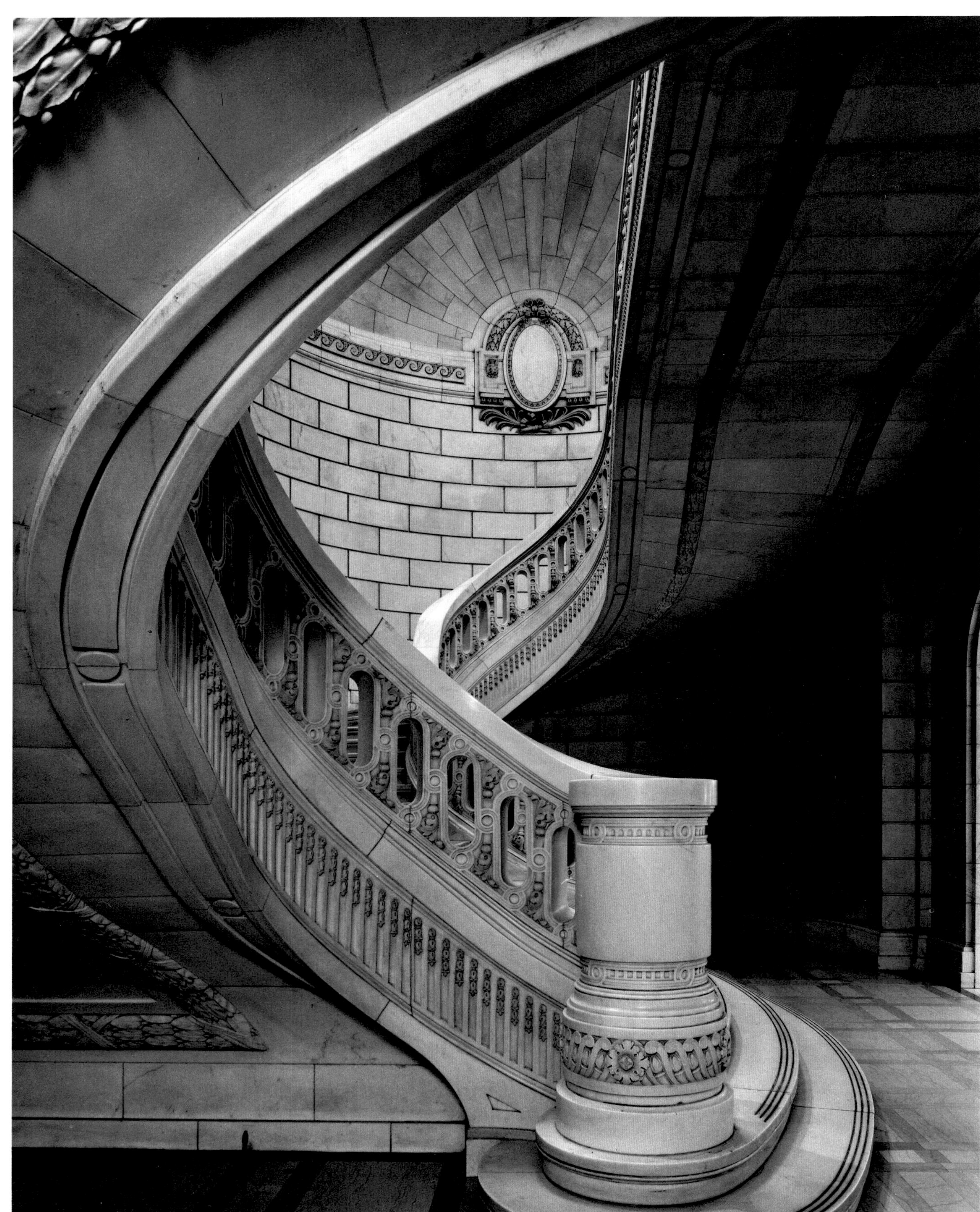

Staircase, Cuyahoga County Courthouse. 1 Lakeside Avenue NW. 1919. Lehman and Schmitt, architects. October 1987.

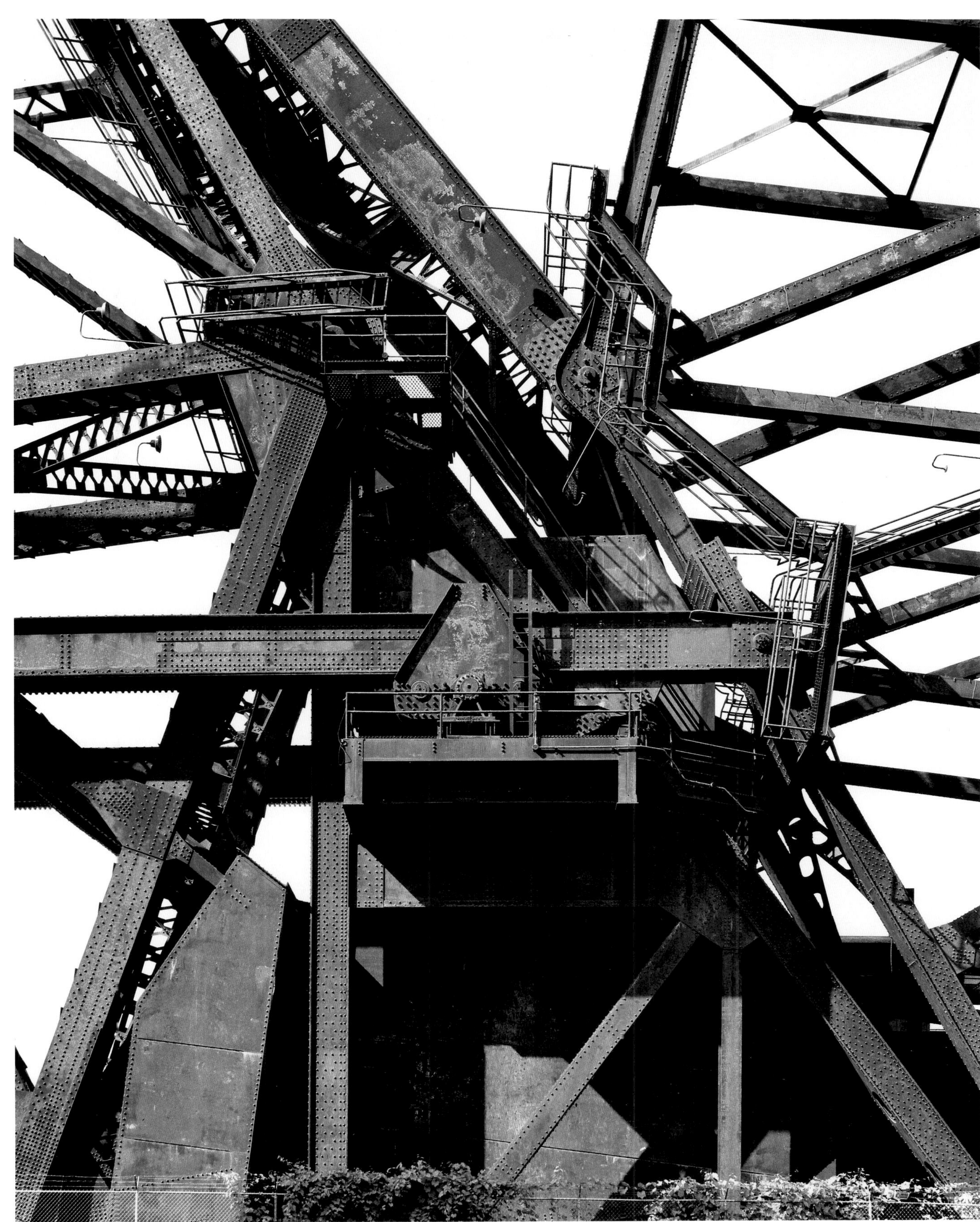

Superior Viaduct at Center Street. 1878. B. F. Morse, engineer. July 1987.

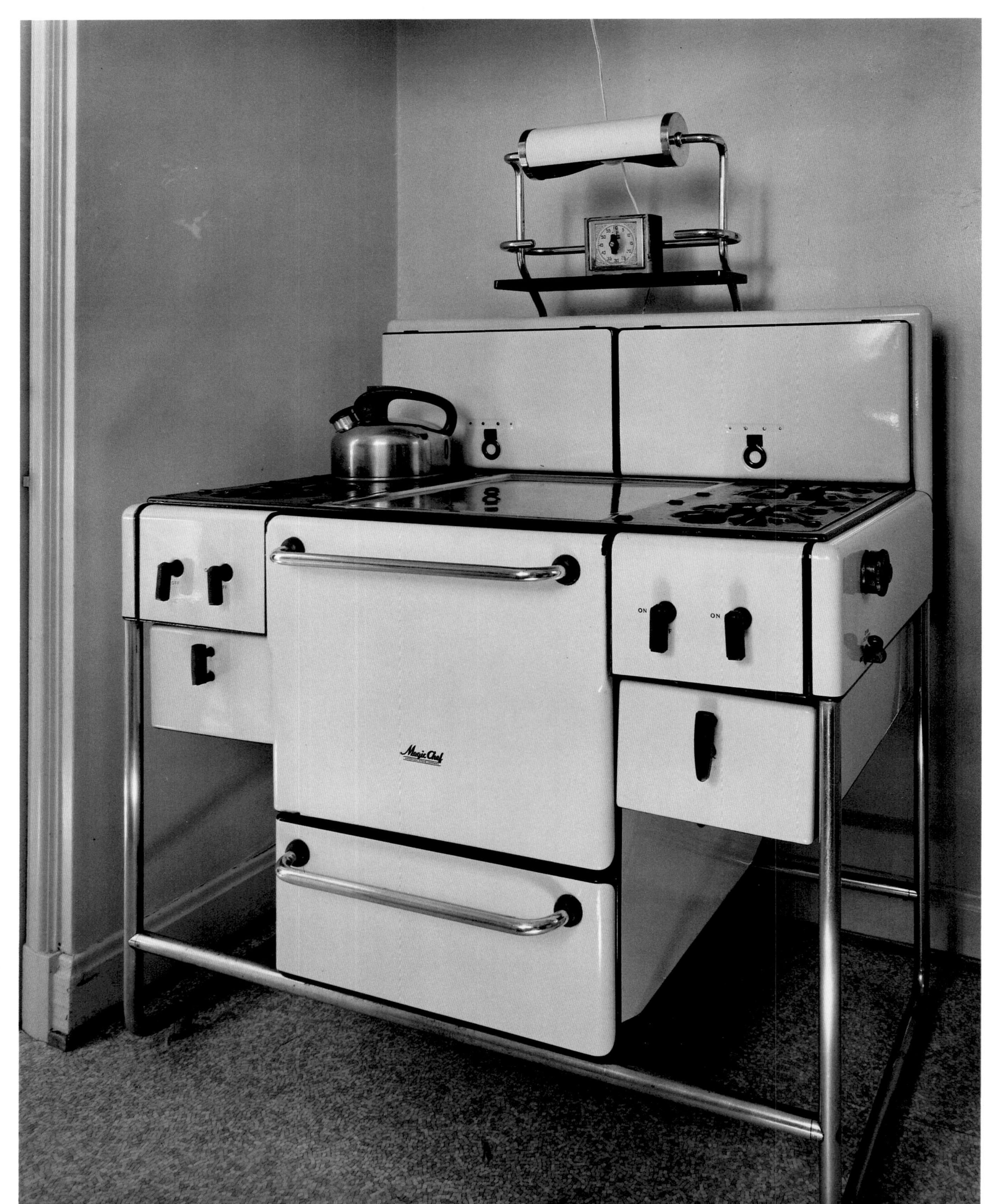

"Magic Chef Stove" (interior of home in "The Belgian Village," originally Fairhill Road village). 12427 Fairhill Road. 1930-31. Harold O. Fullerton, architect. May 1988.

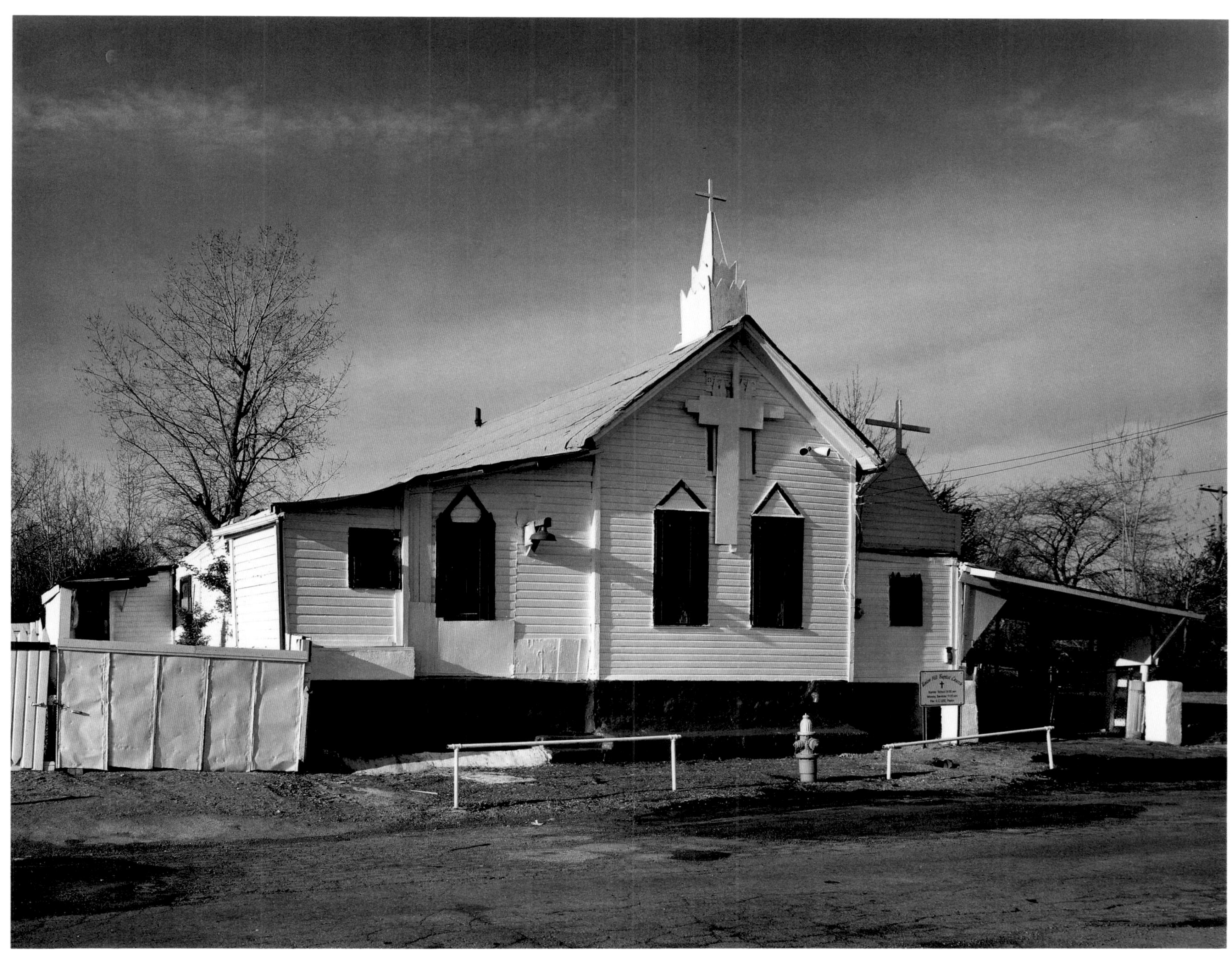

Union Hill Baptist Church. Gill Road and East 83rd Street. Storefront church. May 1988.

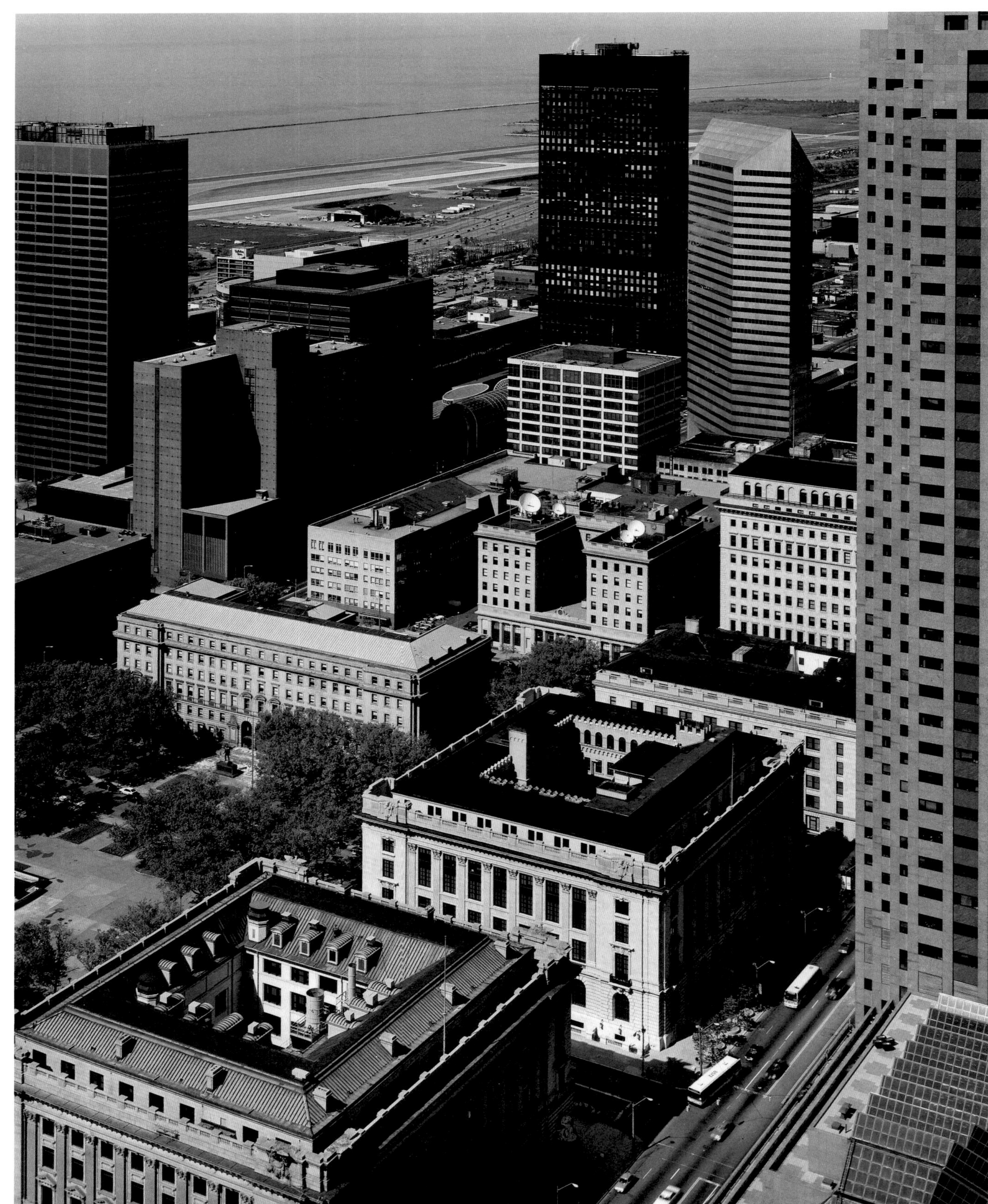

View of Daniel Burnham's 1903 Group Plan with Later Additions Taken From The Terminal Tower. May 1988.

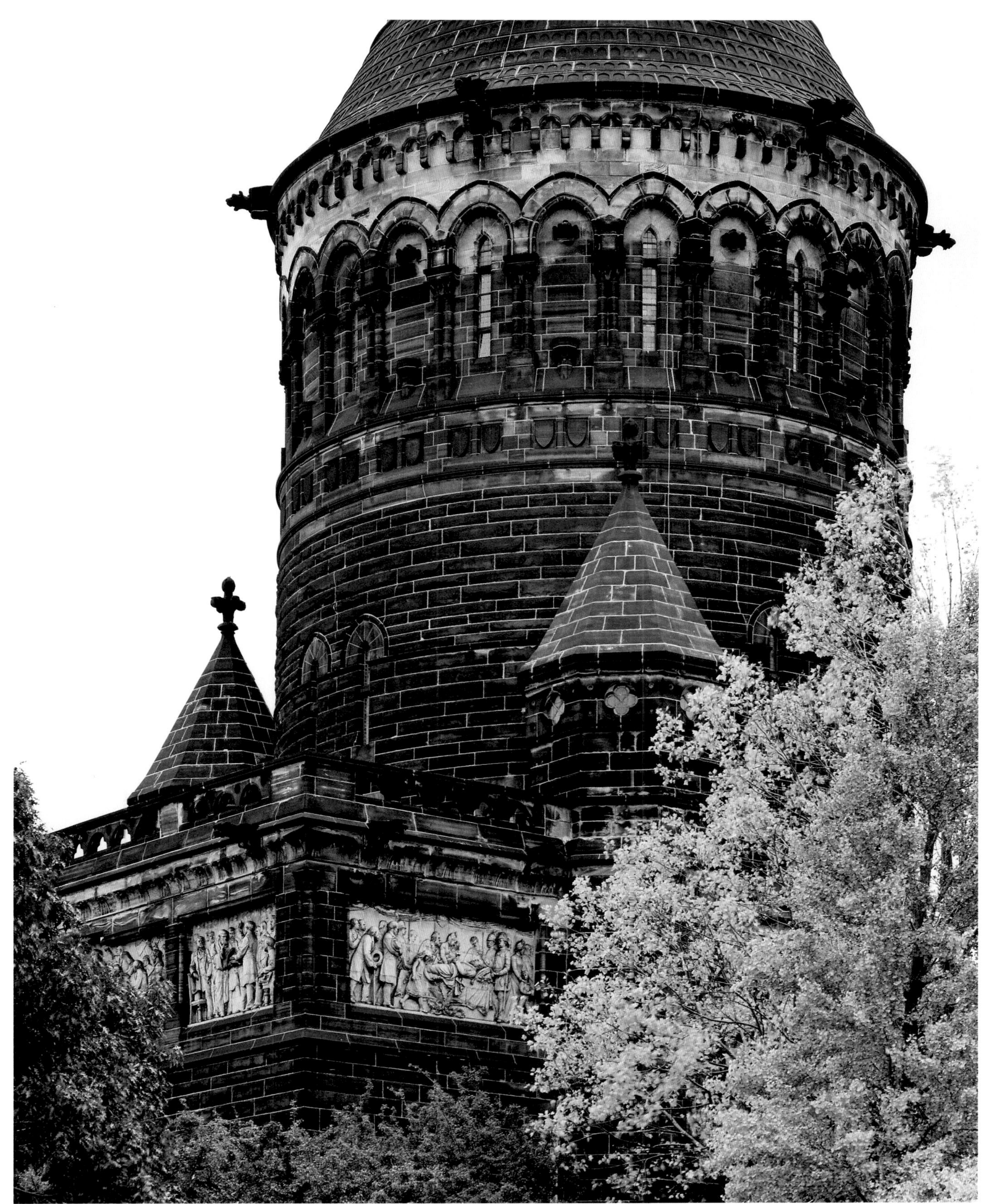

Garfield Monument. Lakeview Cemetery, 12316 Euclid Avenue. 1890. George W. Keller, architect. October 1987.

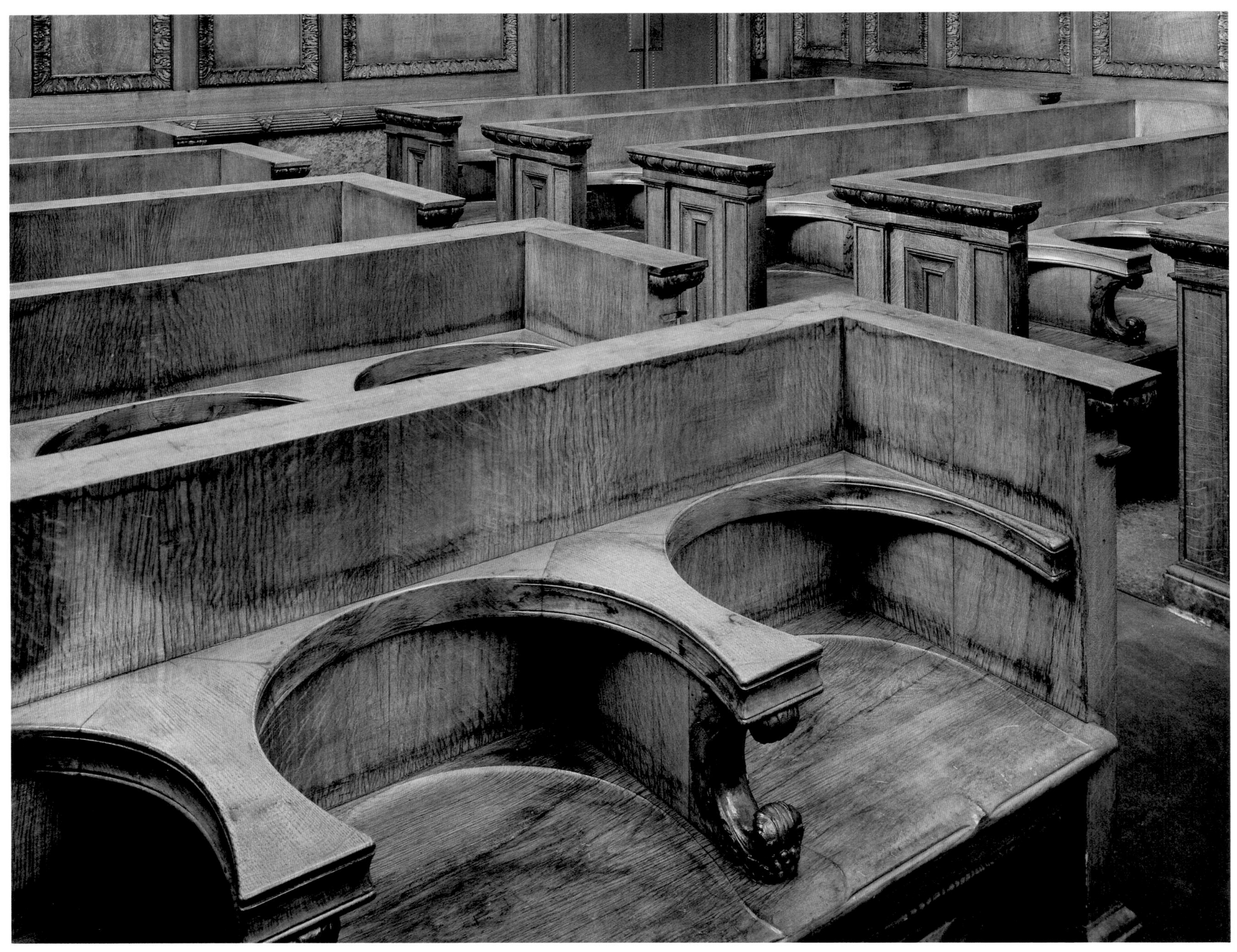

County Appellate Courtroom,
Cuyahoga County Courthouse.
1 Lakeside Avenue NW. 1912.
Lehman and Schmitt, architects.
February 1988.

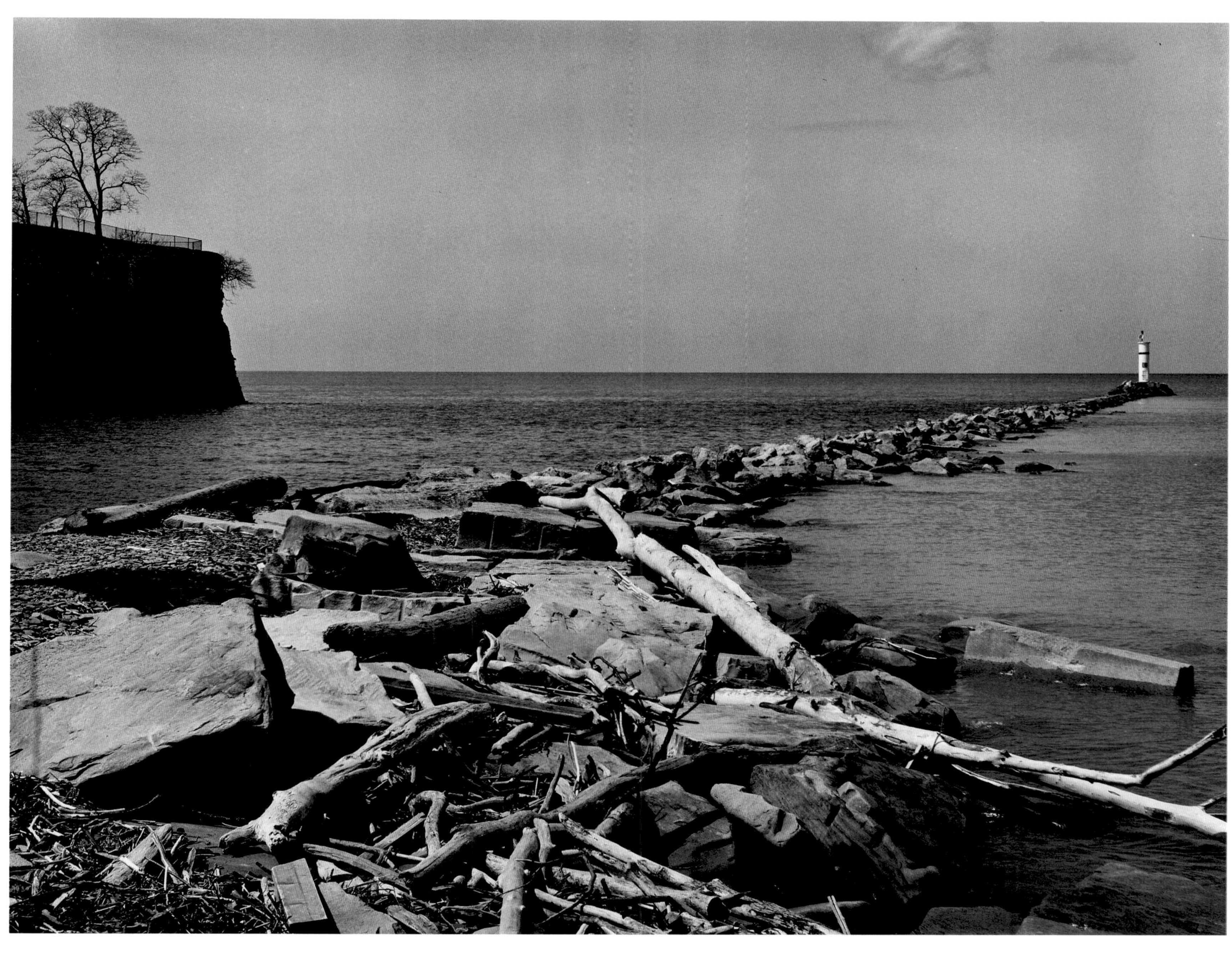

Mouth of the Rocky River as seen from Clifton Beach.
Lakewood. April 1989.

Subjects must be seen as time has marked them.

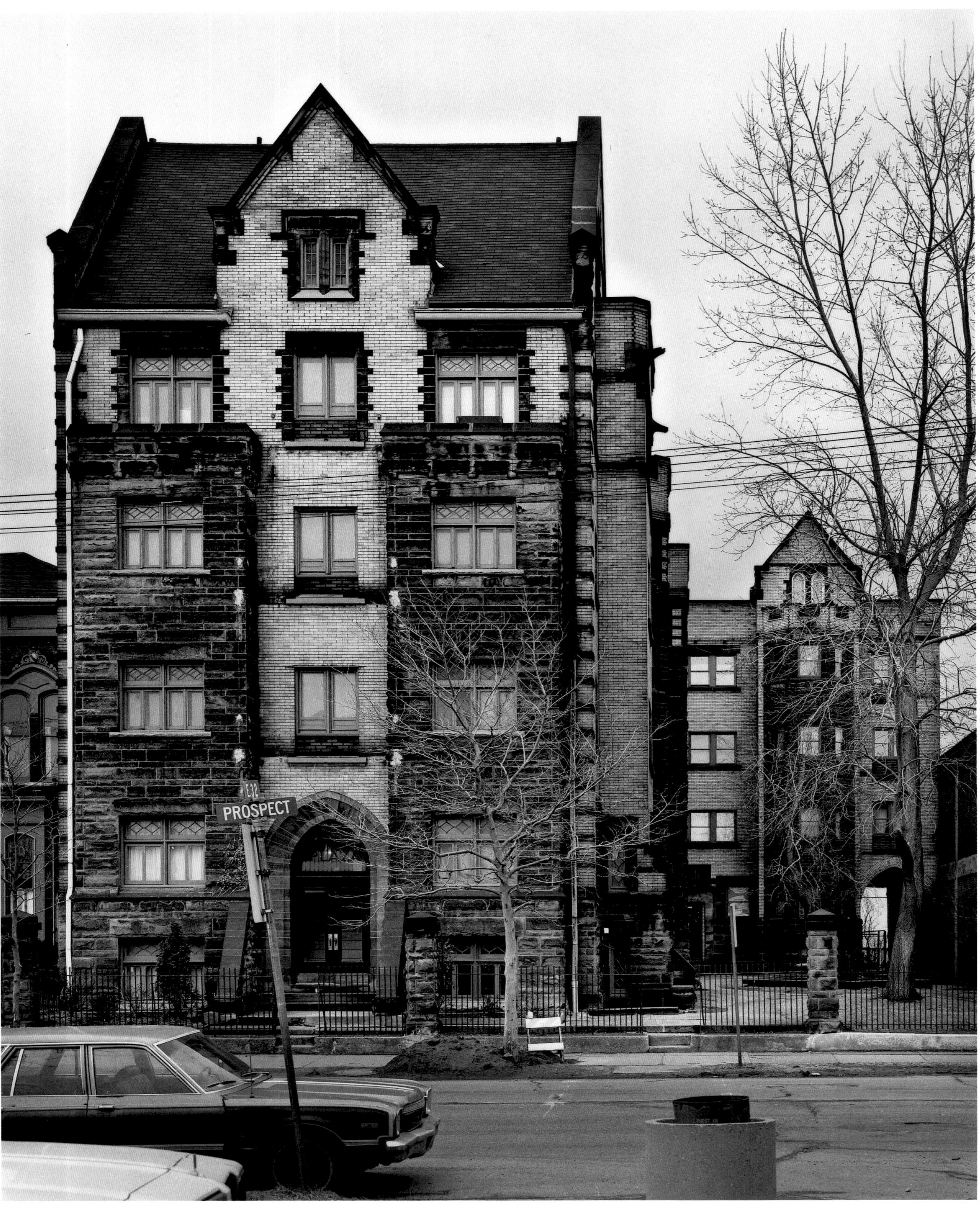

Plaza Apartments. 3206 Prospect Avenue. March 1988.

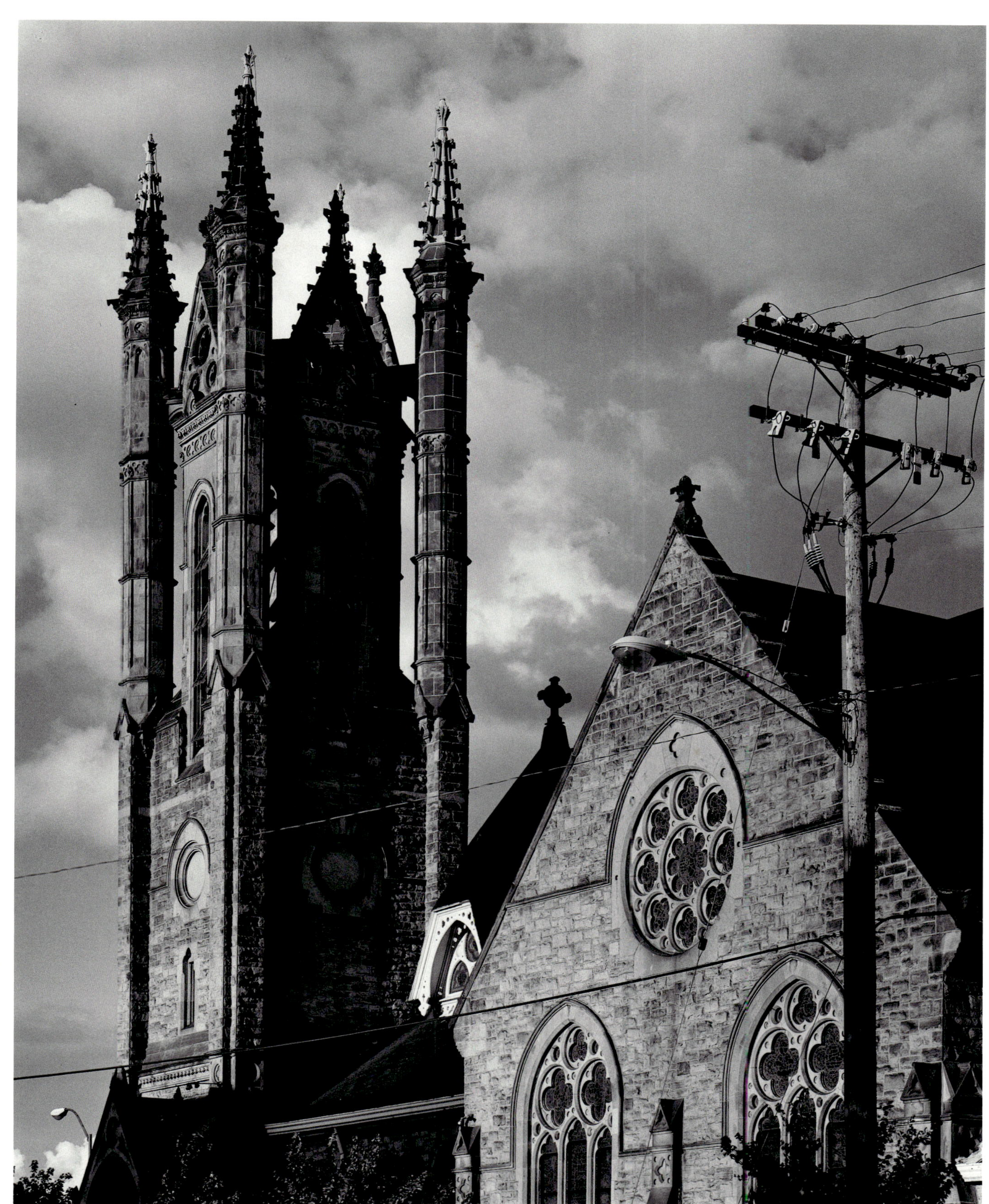

St. Paul Shrine of the Blessed Sacrament (originally St. Paul's Episcopal Church). 4120 Euclid Avenue. 1876. Gordon Floyd, architect. October 1987.

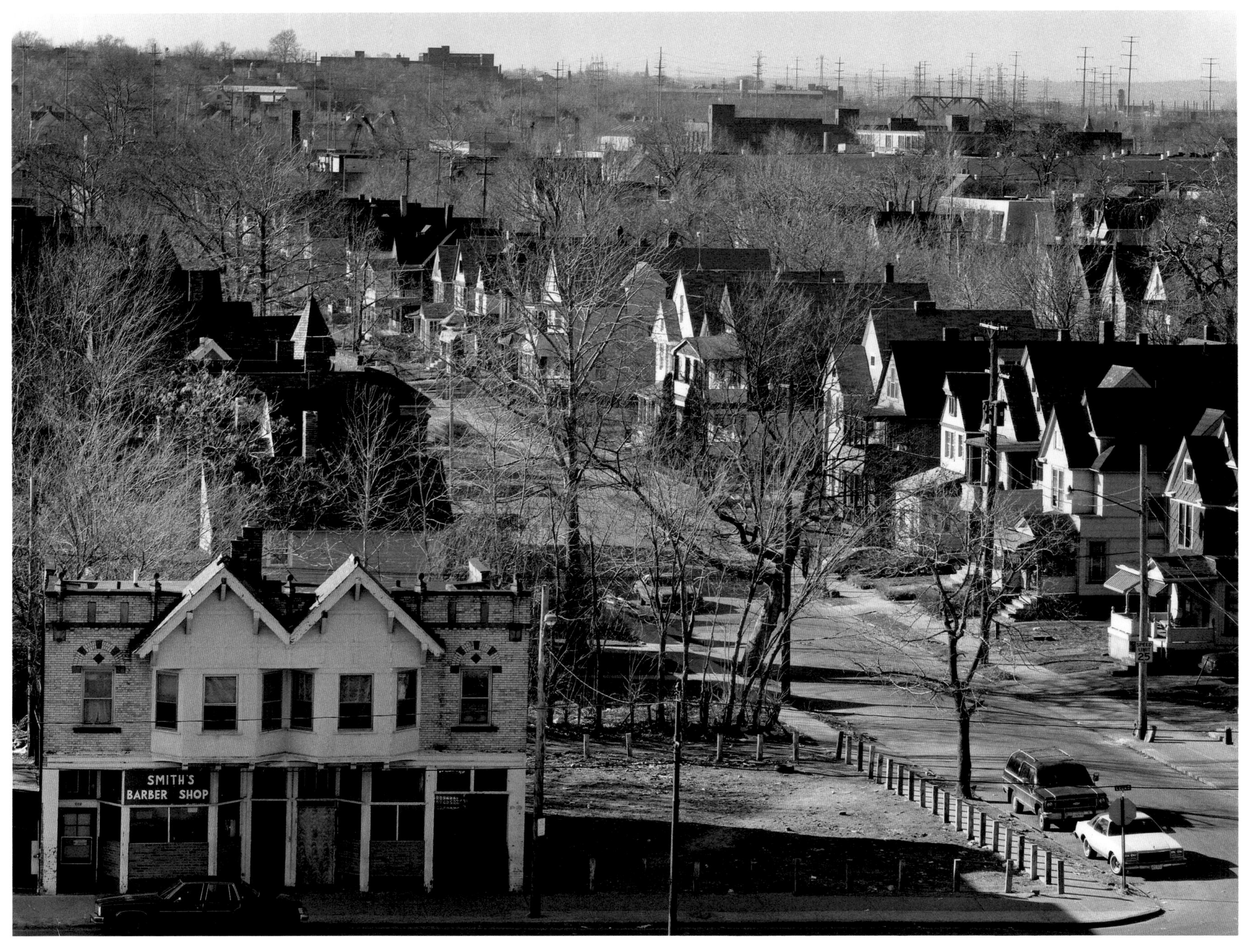

10108 Cedar Road and East 101st Street. View from Cleveland Clinic Parking Garage. March 1988.

D I A L O G U E S

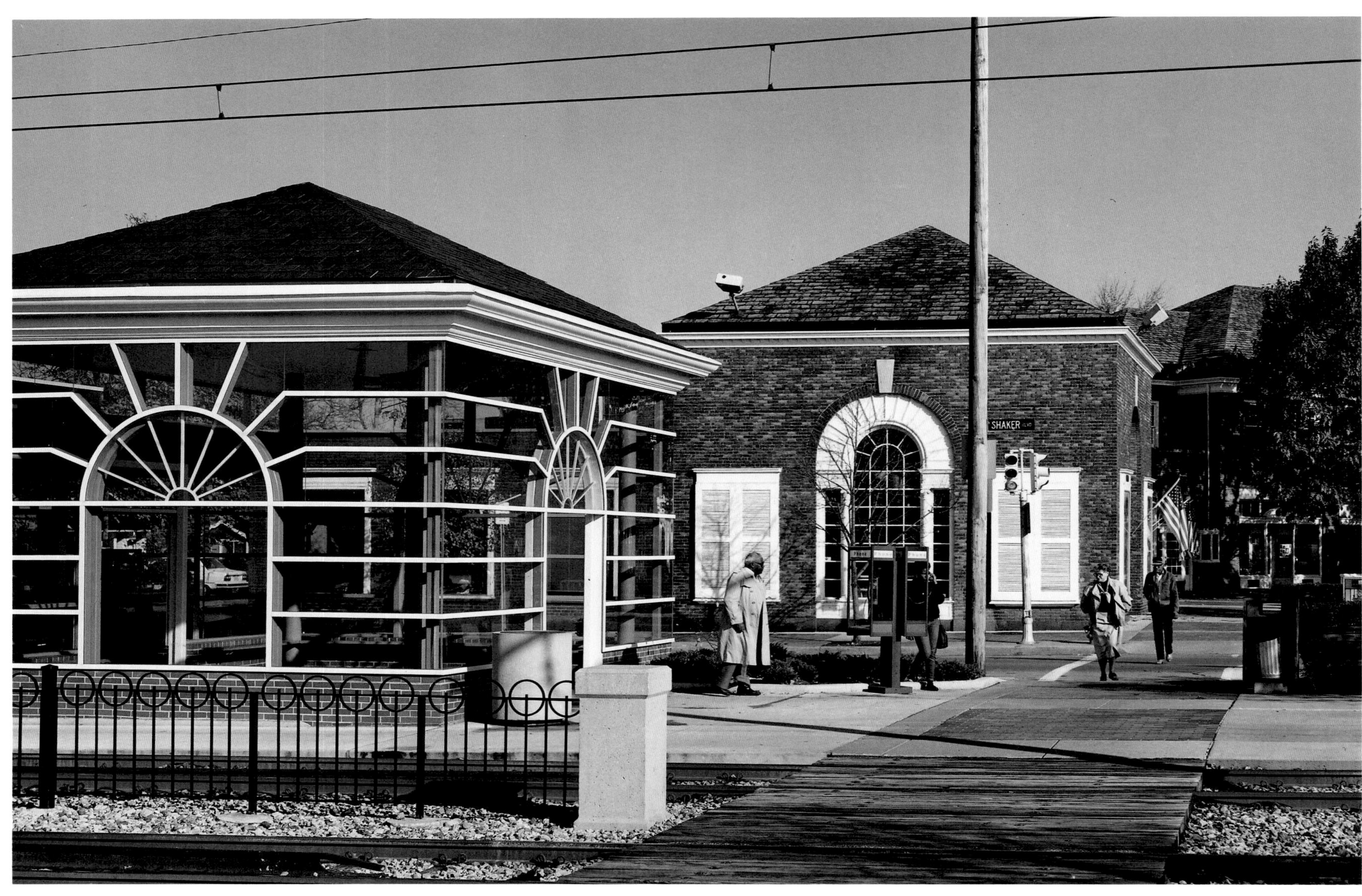

Rapid Transit Authority Stop and Shaker Square. Shaker Square, Shaker Heights. Left foreground: R.T.A. Stop. 1985. Gould Associates and Milky Brown, architects and engineer. Right background: Shaker Square. 1927-29. Small and Rowley, architects. October 1987.

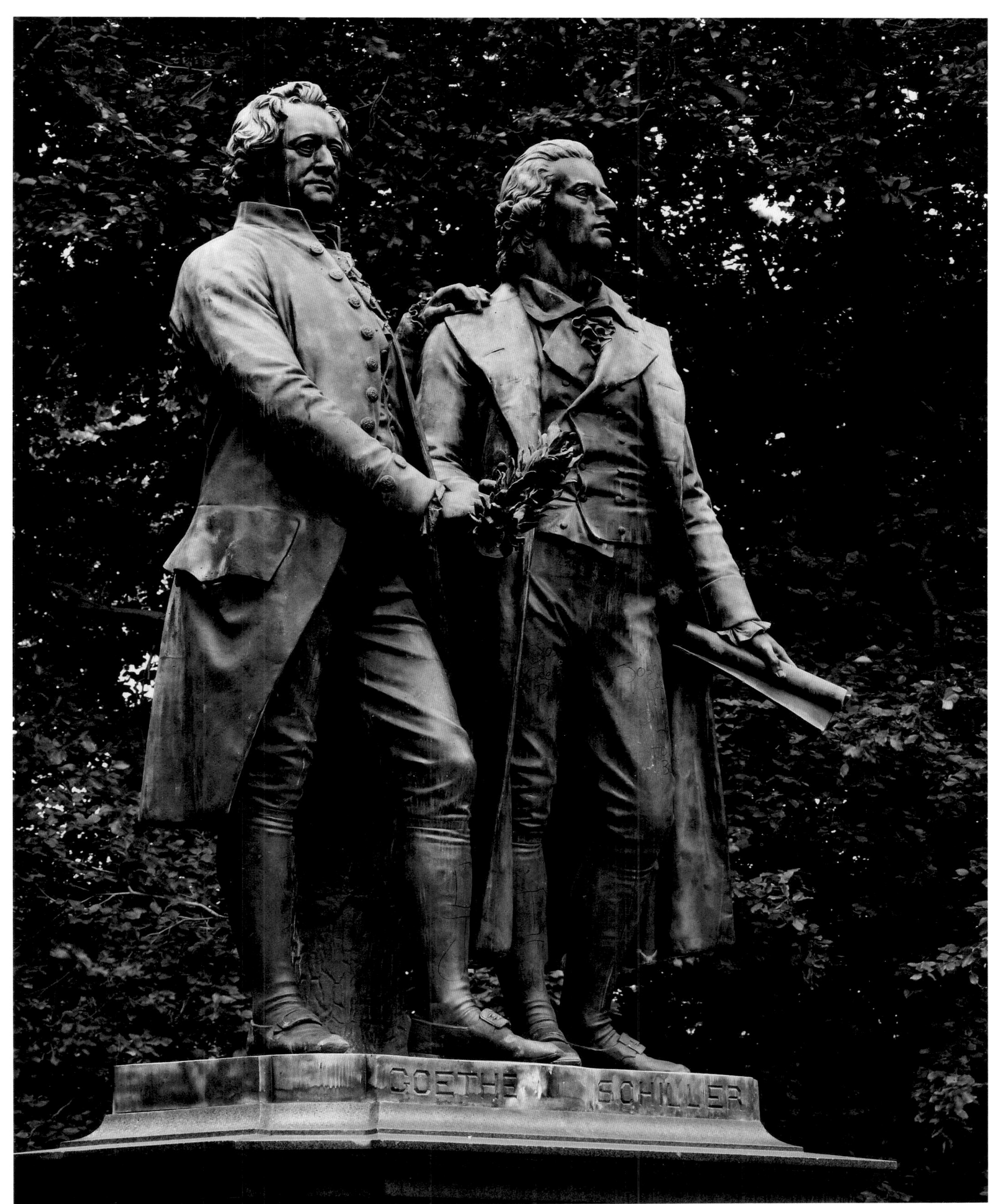

"Goethe and Schiller," German Cultural Garden. East and North Boulevards. 1929. Herman Dercum, architect. The sculpture is a replica of the original in Weimar, Germany. September 1987.

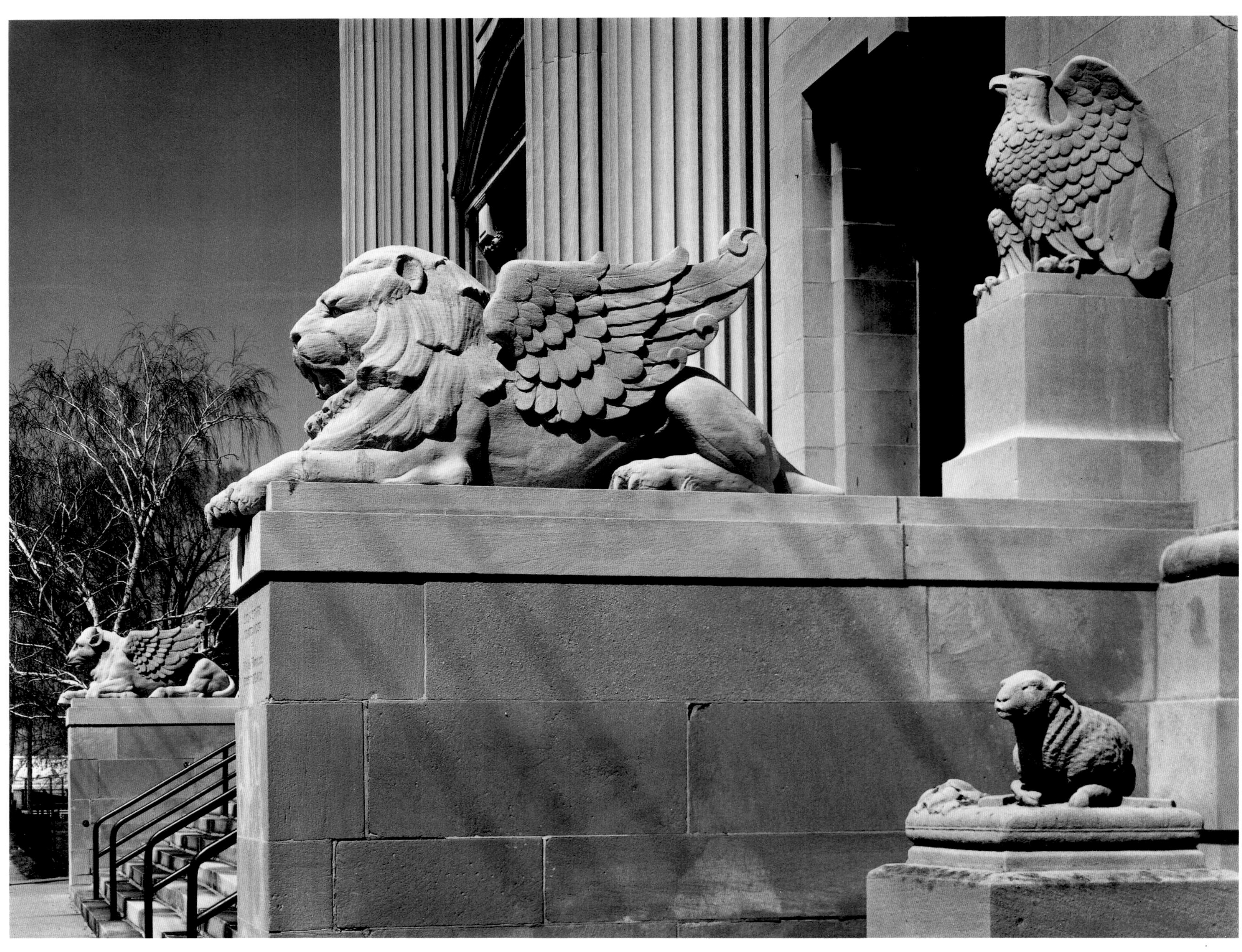

St. Colman's Roman Catholic Church. 2027 West 65th Street. 1918. Attributed to William Ginther, architect. April 1989.

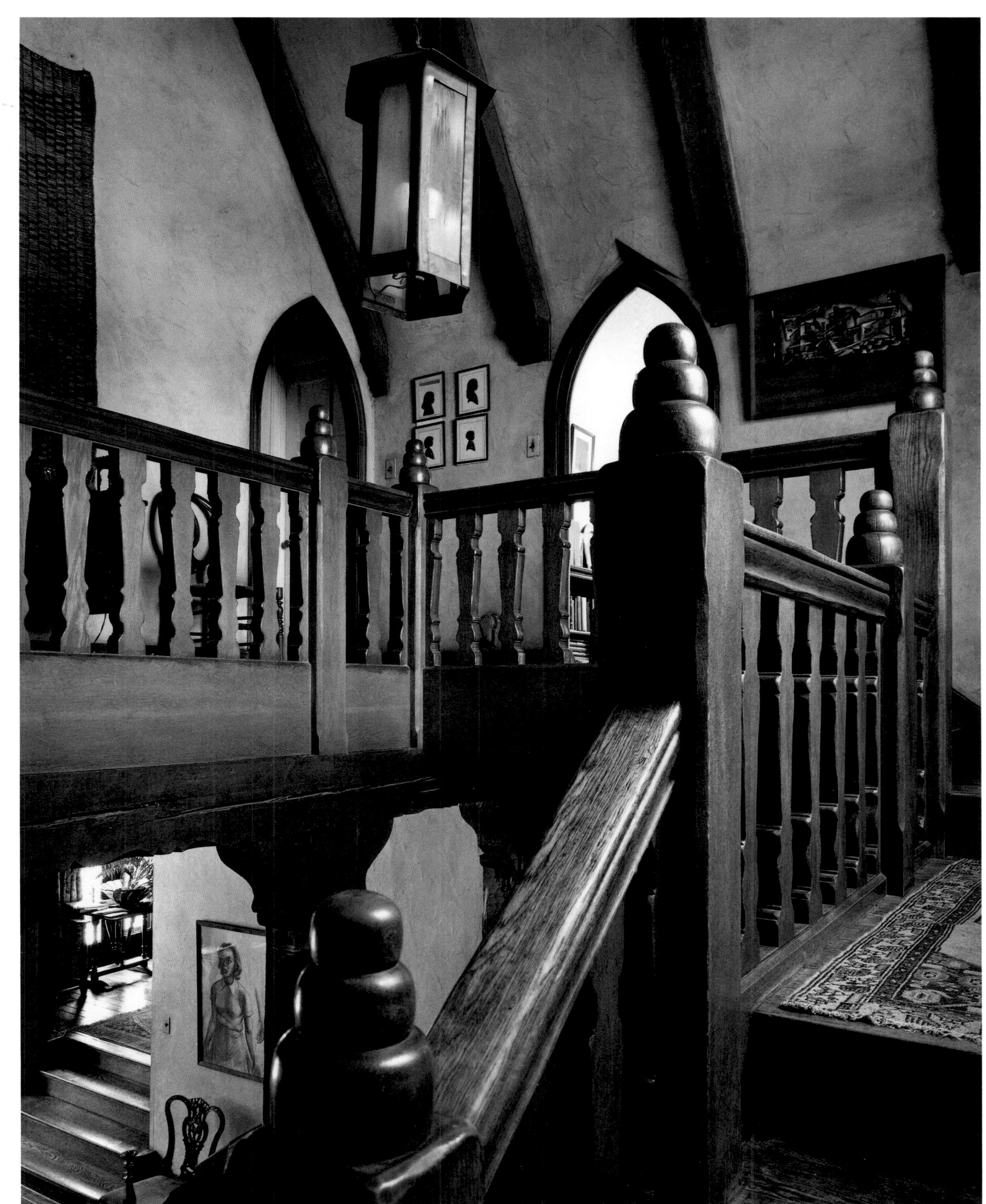

Staircase, Home in ''The Belgian Village'' (originally Fairhill Road village). 12427 Fairhill Road. 1930-31. Harold O. Fullerton, architect. May 1988.

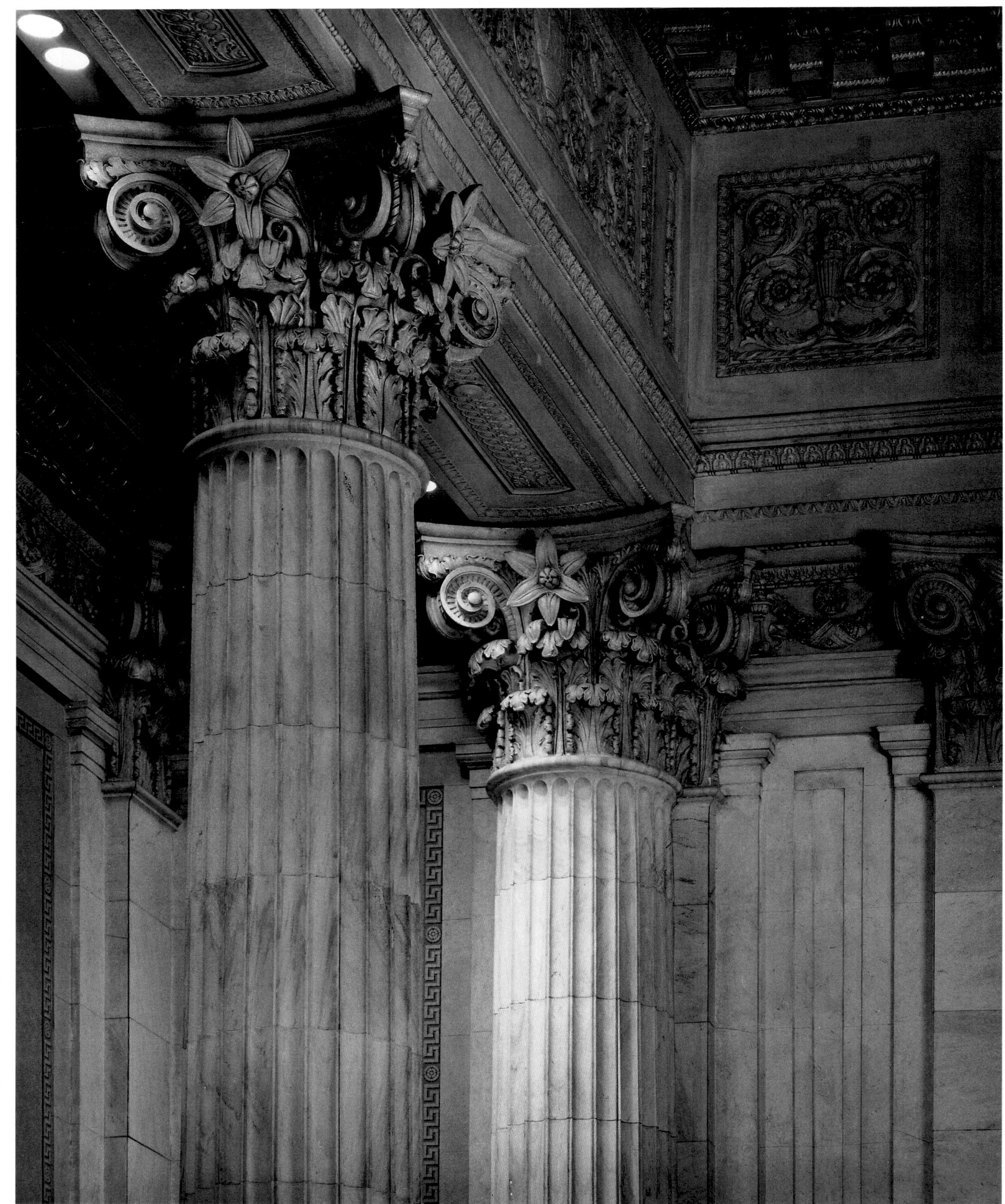

Corinthian Capitals, Main Banking Hall, Old National City Bank Building (originally New England Building, later Guardian Bank Building). 1896. Shepley, Rutan, and Coolidge, architects. Façade altered and main banking hall remodeled 1915. Walker and Weeks, architects. October 1987.

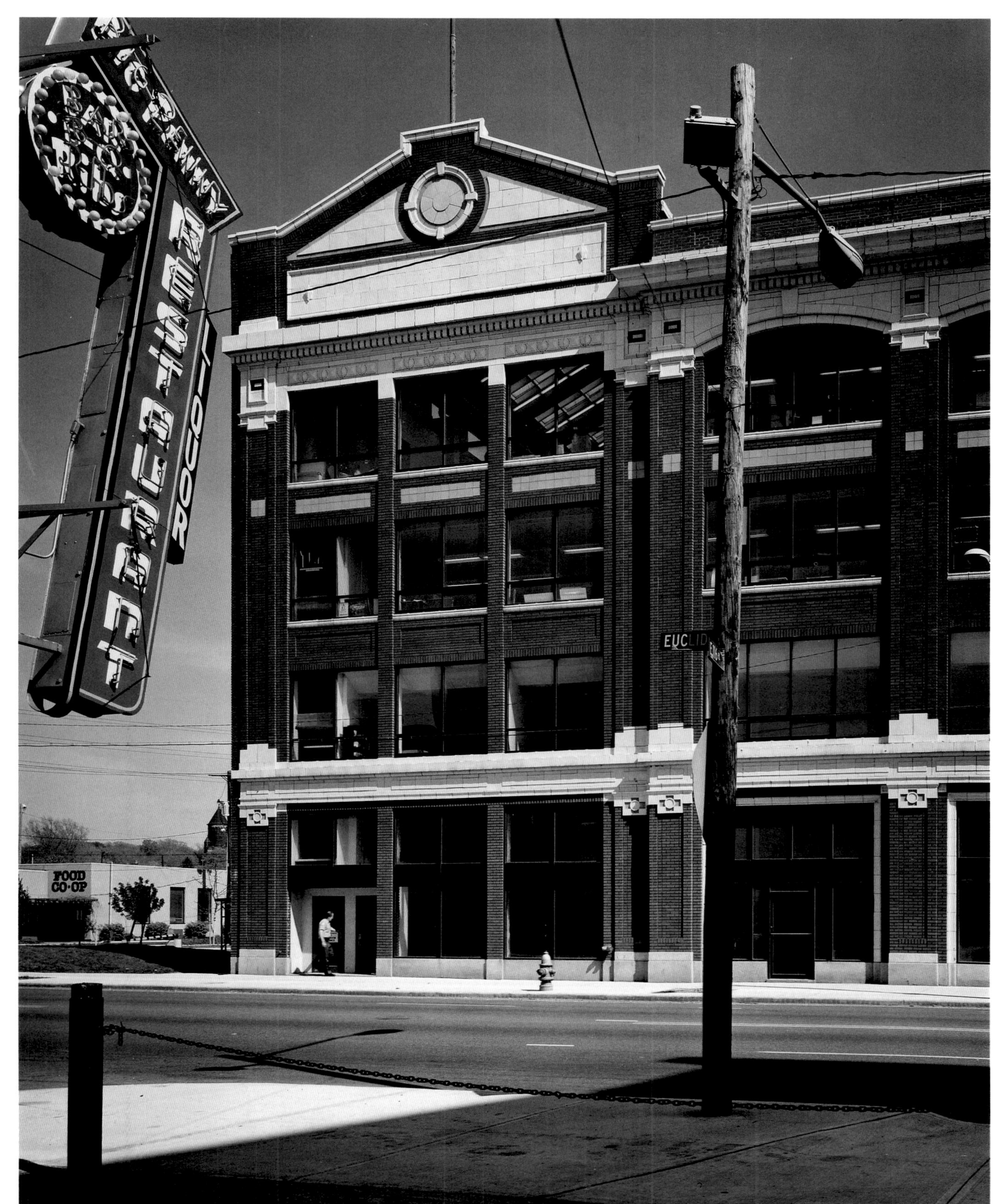

Cleveland Institute of Art Factory (originally Ford Motor Company Branch Assembly Plant). 11610 Euclid Avenue. 1914. Albert Kahn, architect. May 1988.

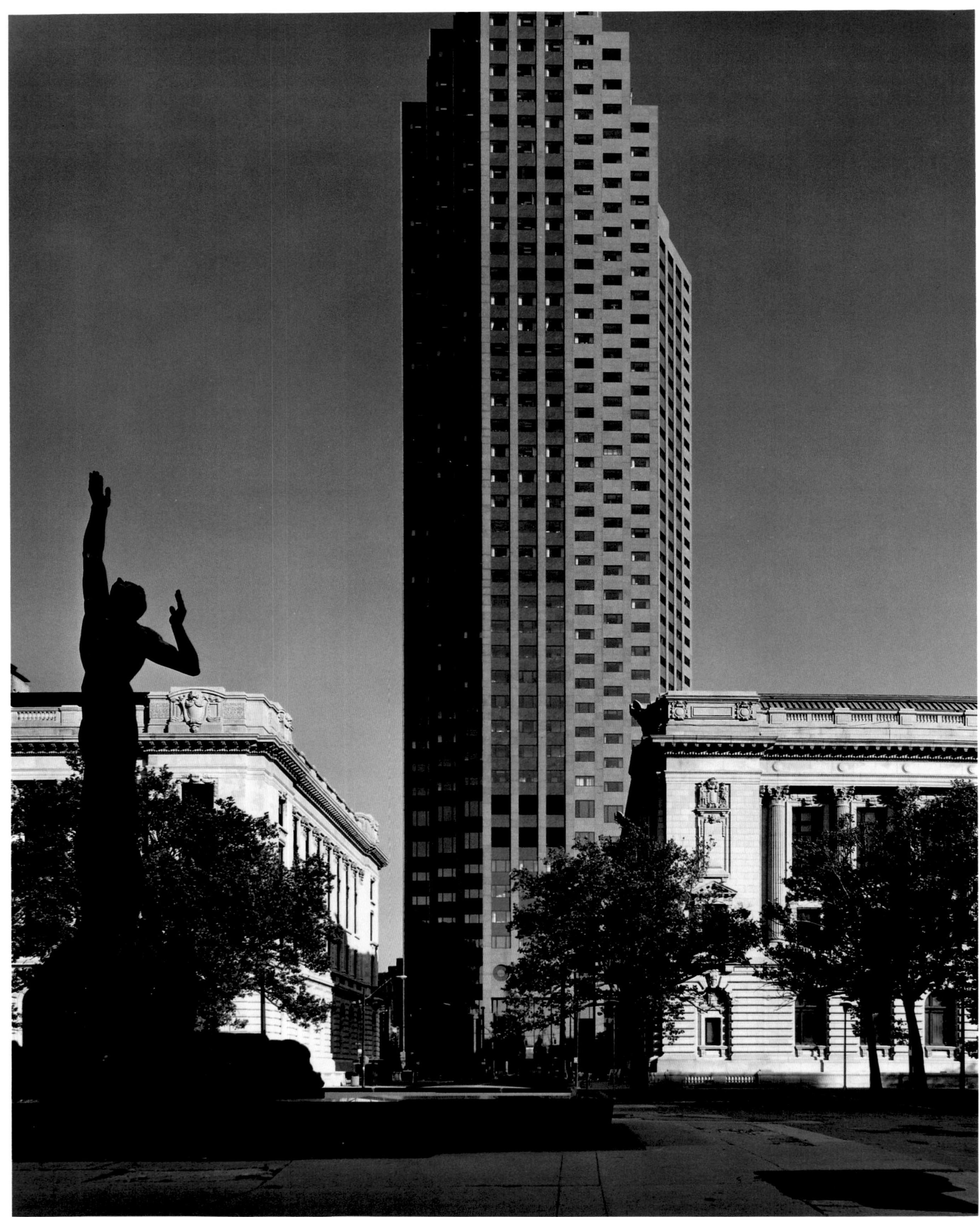

South End of Daniel Burnham's 1903 Group Plan with World War I Monument (foreground), *Cleveland Public Library* (left), *BP America Building* (center), *and The Federal Building* (right). "The Eternal Life," World War I monument by Marshall Fredericks, sculptor. Commissioned 1946. Cleveland Public Library erected 1925. Walker and Weeks, architects. BP America Headquarters Building opened 1985. Gyo Obata, architect. The Federal Building (originally U.S. Post Office, Custom House, and Court House) erected 1910. Arnold W. Brunner, architect. July 1988.

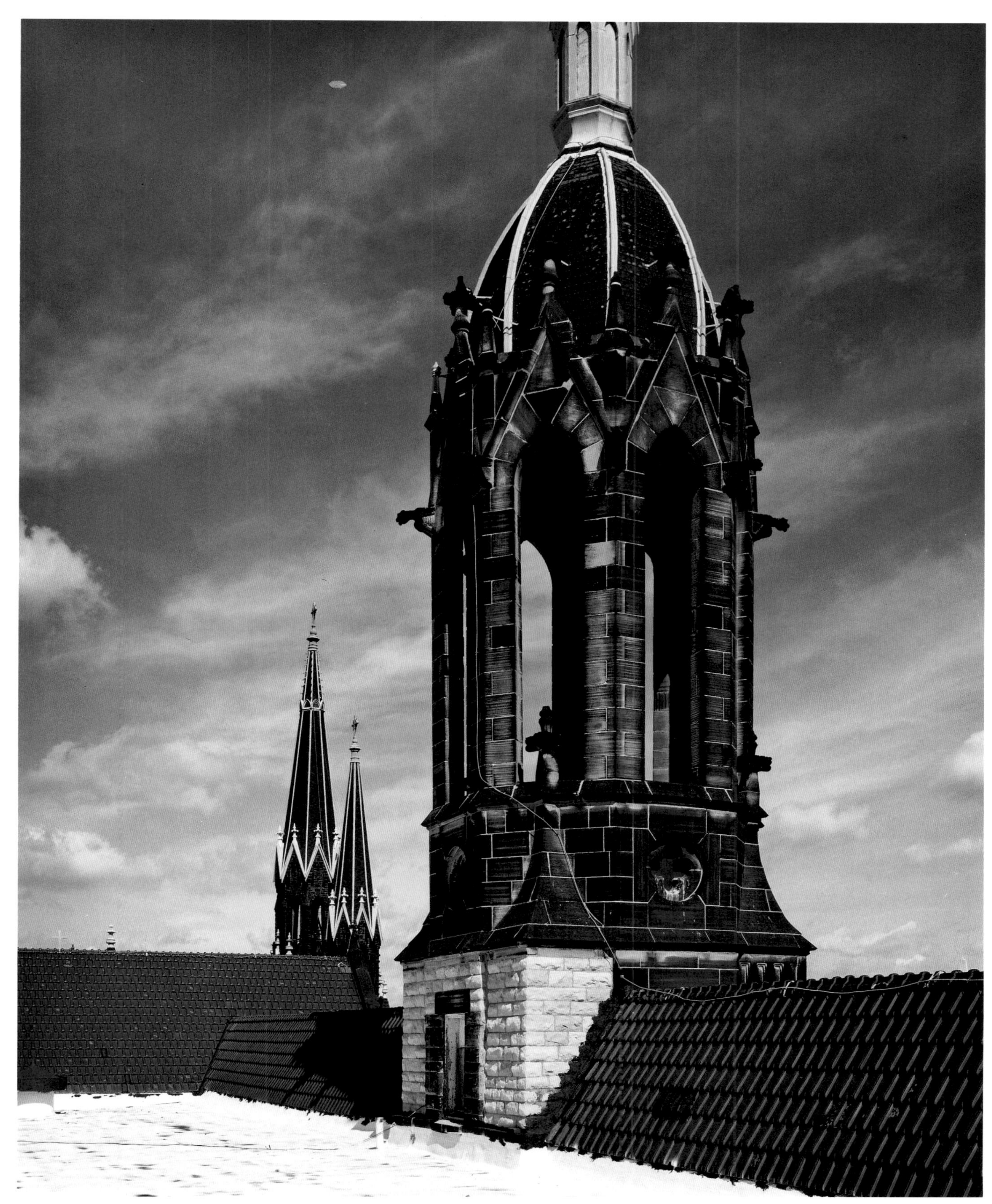

St. Michael's Roman Catholic Convent School. 2202 Prame Avenue. 1906. Emile Uhlrich, architect. September 1987.

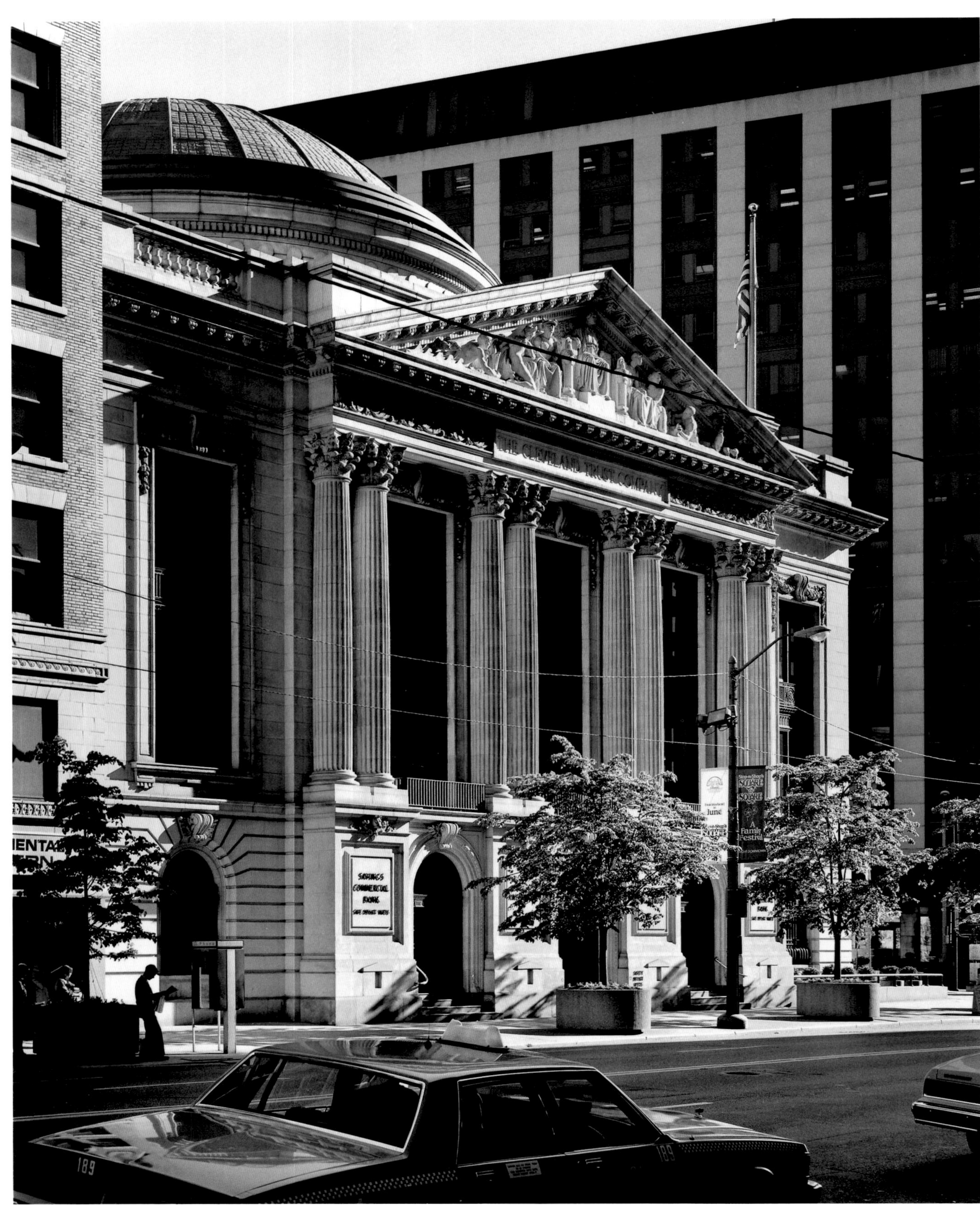

Ameritrust Building (originally The Cleveland Trust Company). 900 Euclid Avenue. 1908. George B. Post and Sons, architects. May 1988.

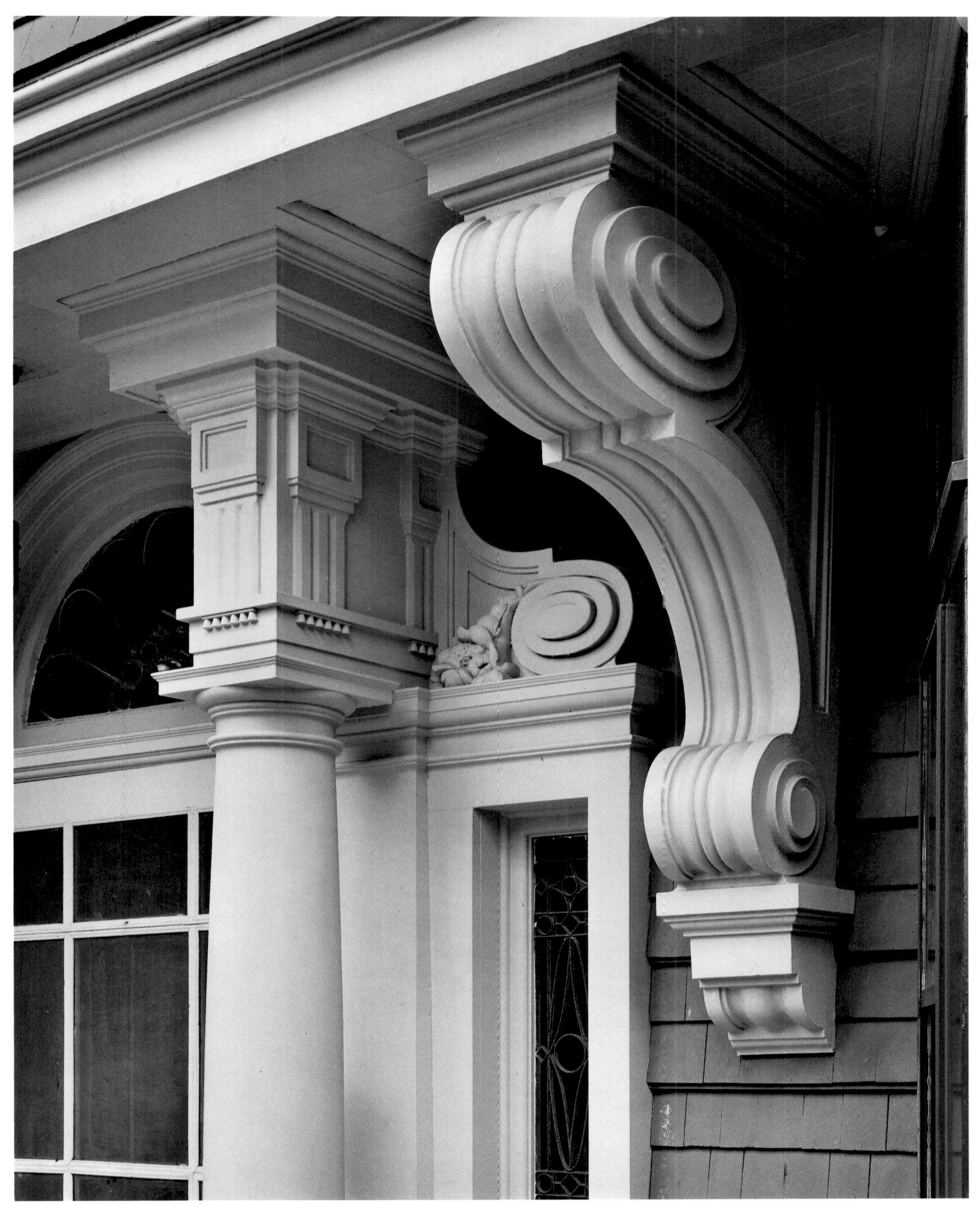

2720 East Overlook Road. Cleveland Heights. October 1987.

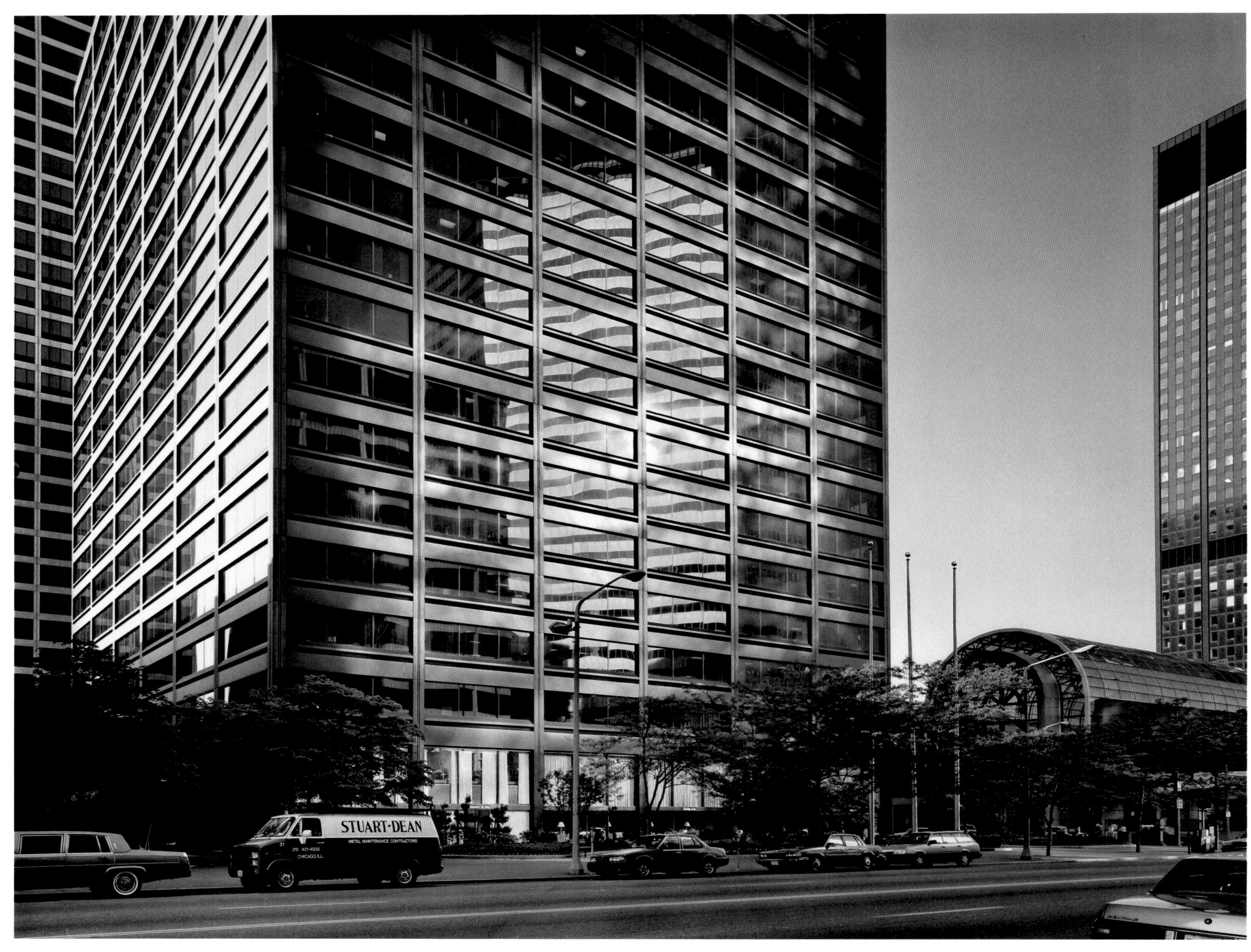

Bond Court Office Building. (left). 1300 East 9th Street. 1971. Skidmore, Owings, and Merrill, architects. *The Galleria at Erieview* (right). 1301 East 9th Street. 1987. Kober/Belluschi, Associates Inc., architects. May 1988.

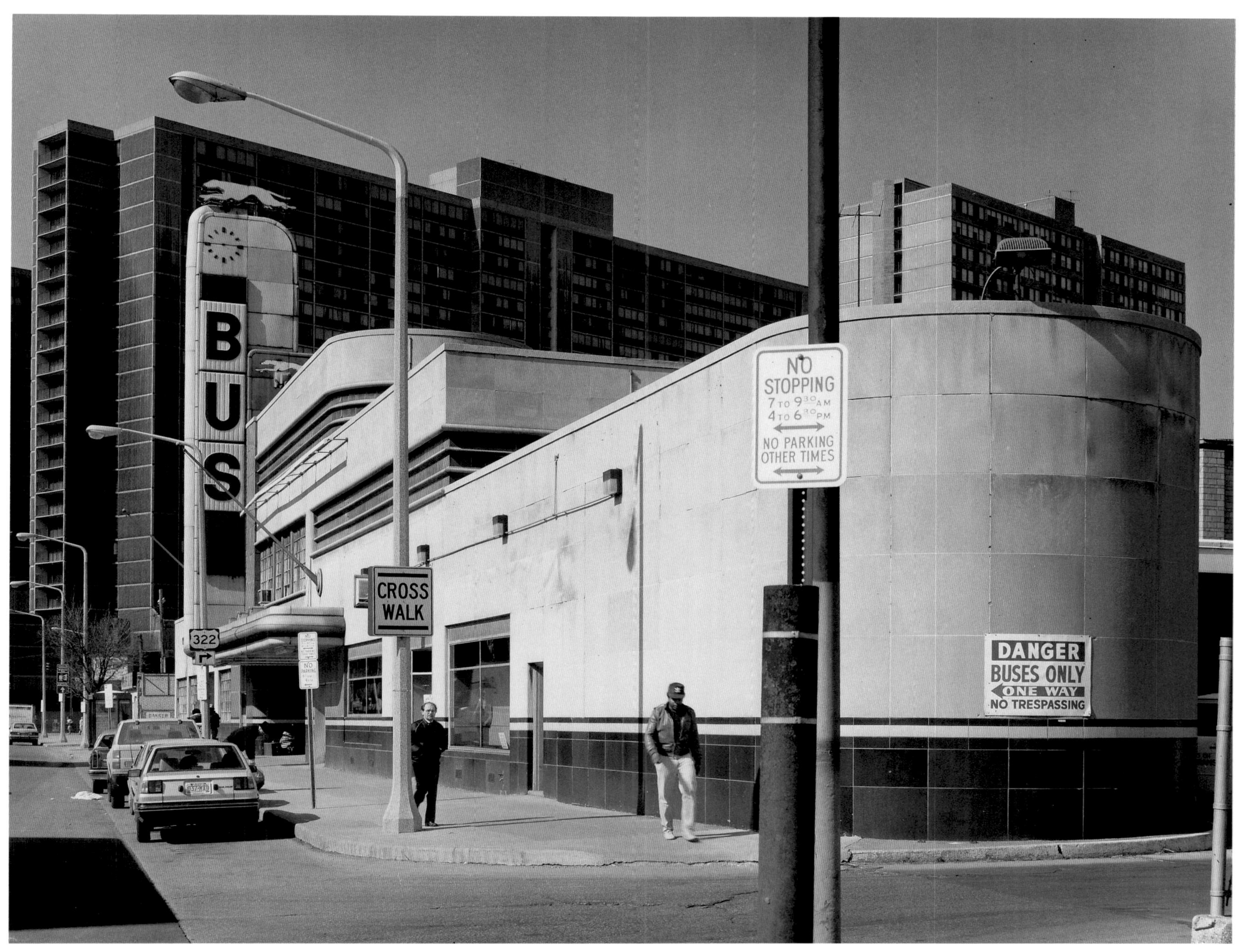

Greyhound Bus Terminal. 1465 Chester Avenue. 1948. W. S. Arrasmith, architect. March 1988.

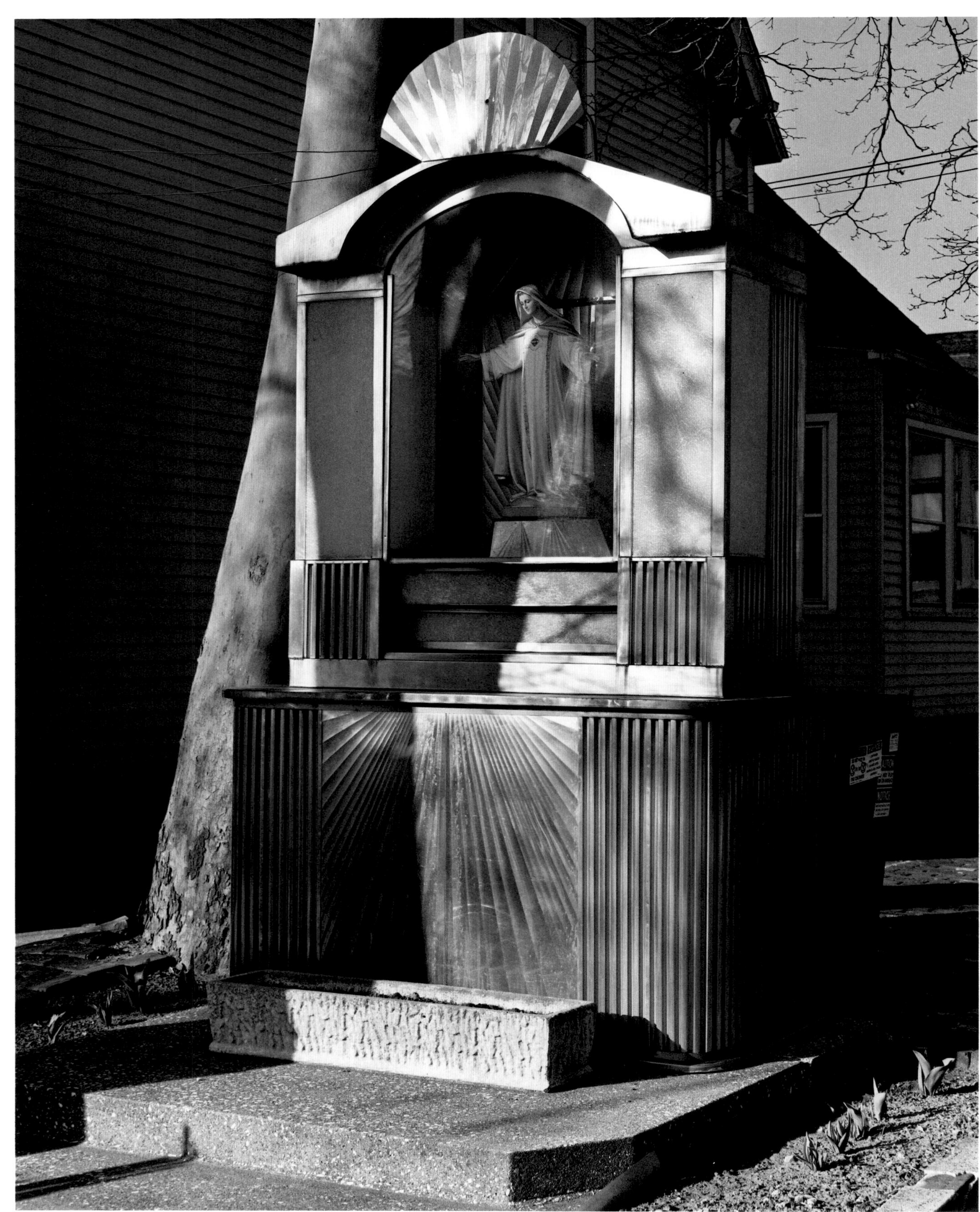

Shrine to Virgin Mary. 1411 East 33rd Street, next to St. Josaphat Roman Catholic Church. Shrine erected 1960. April 1989.

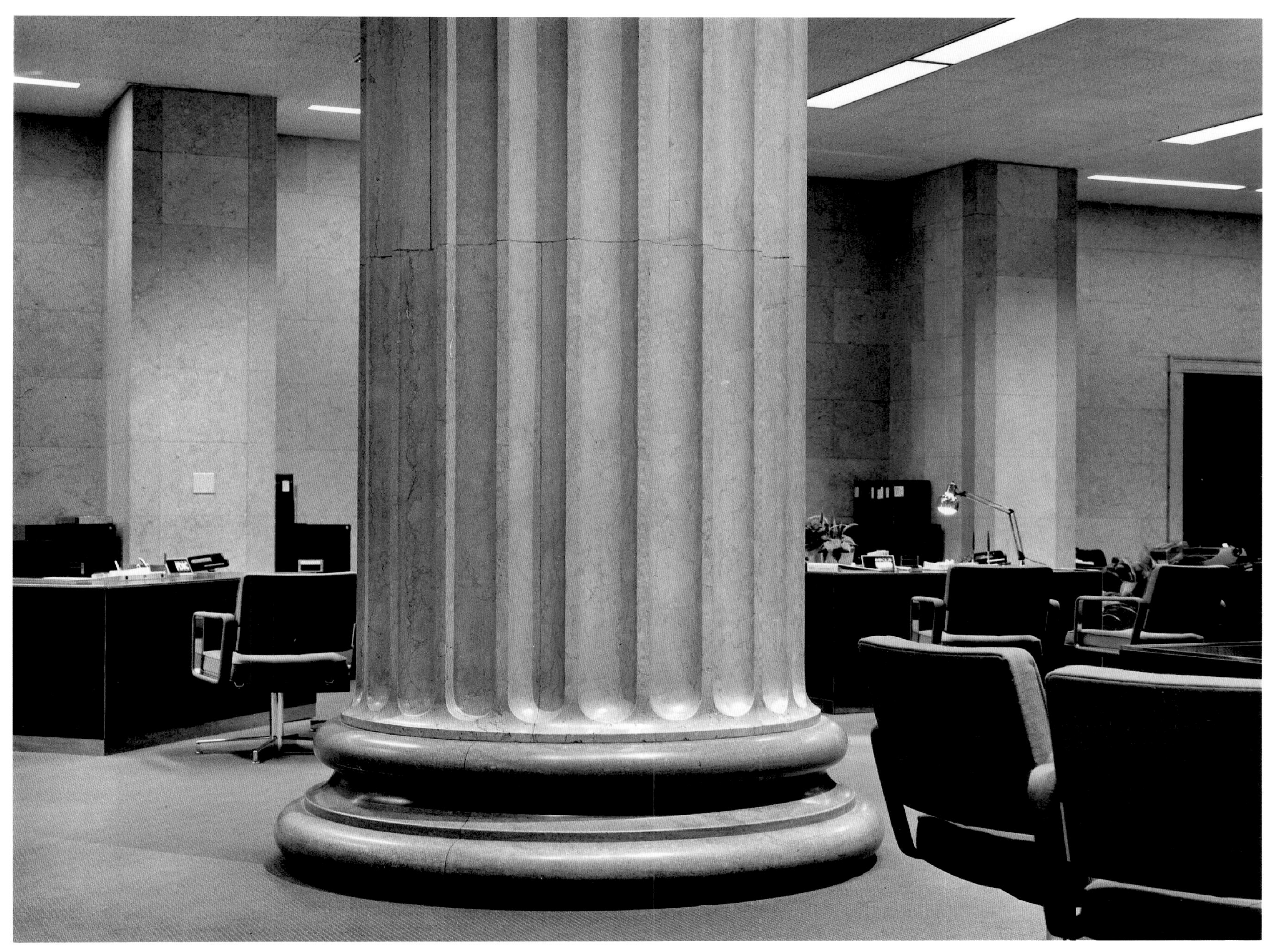

Columns, Main Banking Hall, Huntington Bank Building (originally Union Trust Building, later Union Commerce Bank). 917 Euclid Avenue. 1924. Graham, Anderson, Probst and White, architects; remodeled for Union Commerce Bank by Dalton, van Dijk, Johnson and Partners. February 1988.

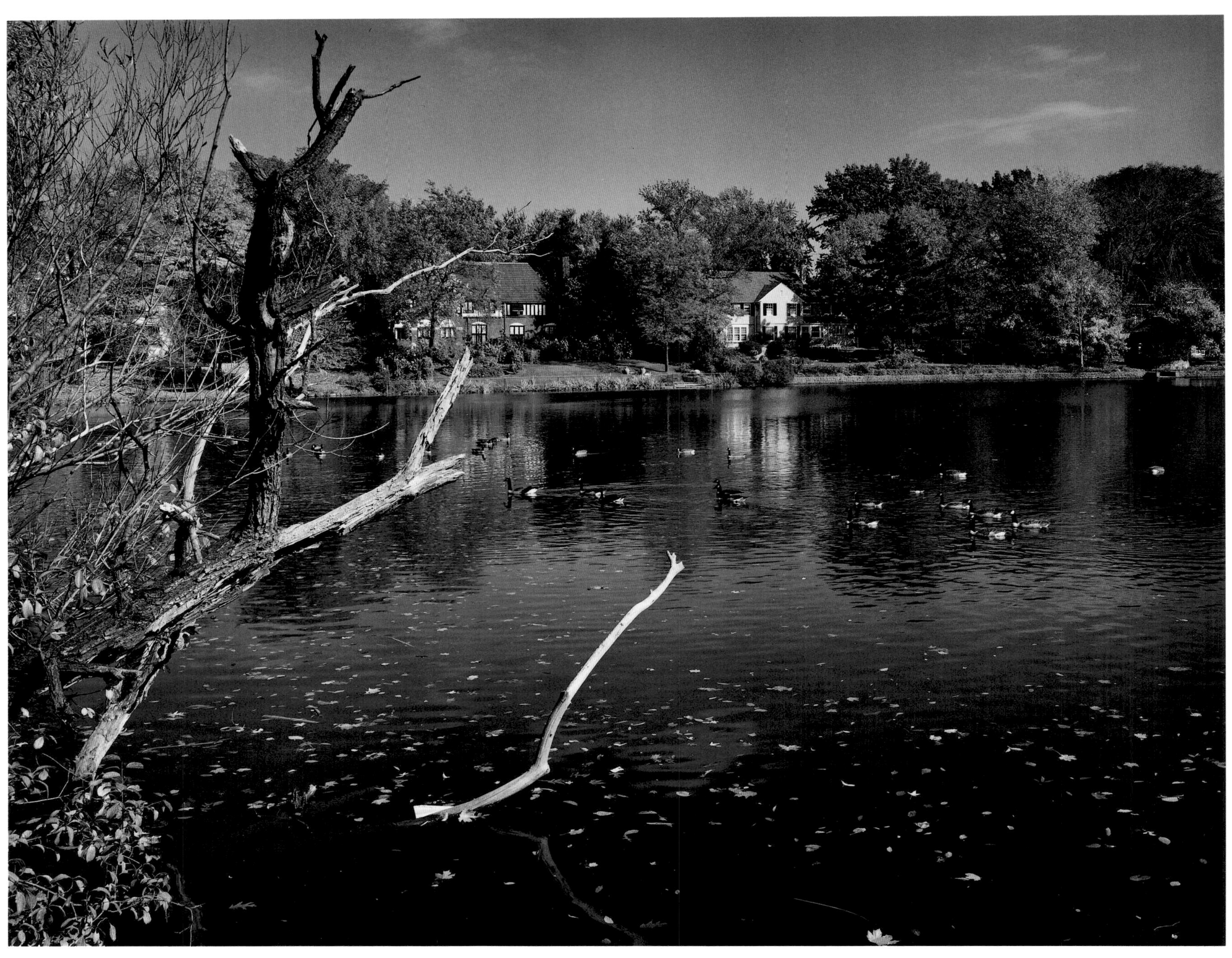

View of Shaker Lakes and Residential Area from Andover Road. Landscaped ca. 1895. Ernest W. Bowditch, landscape architect. October 1987.

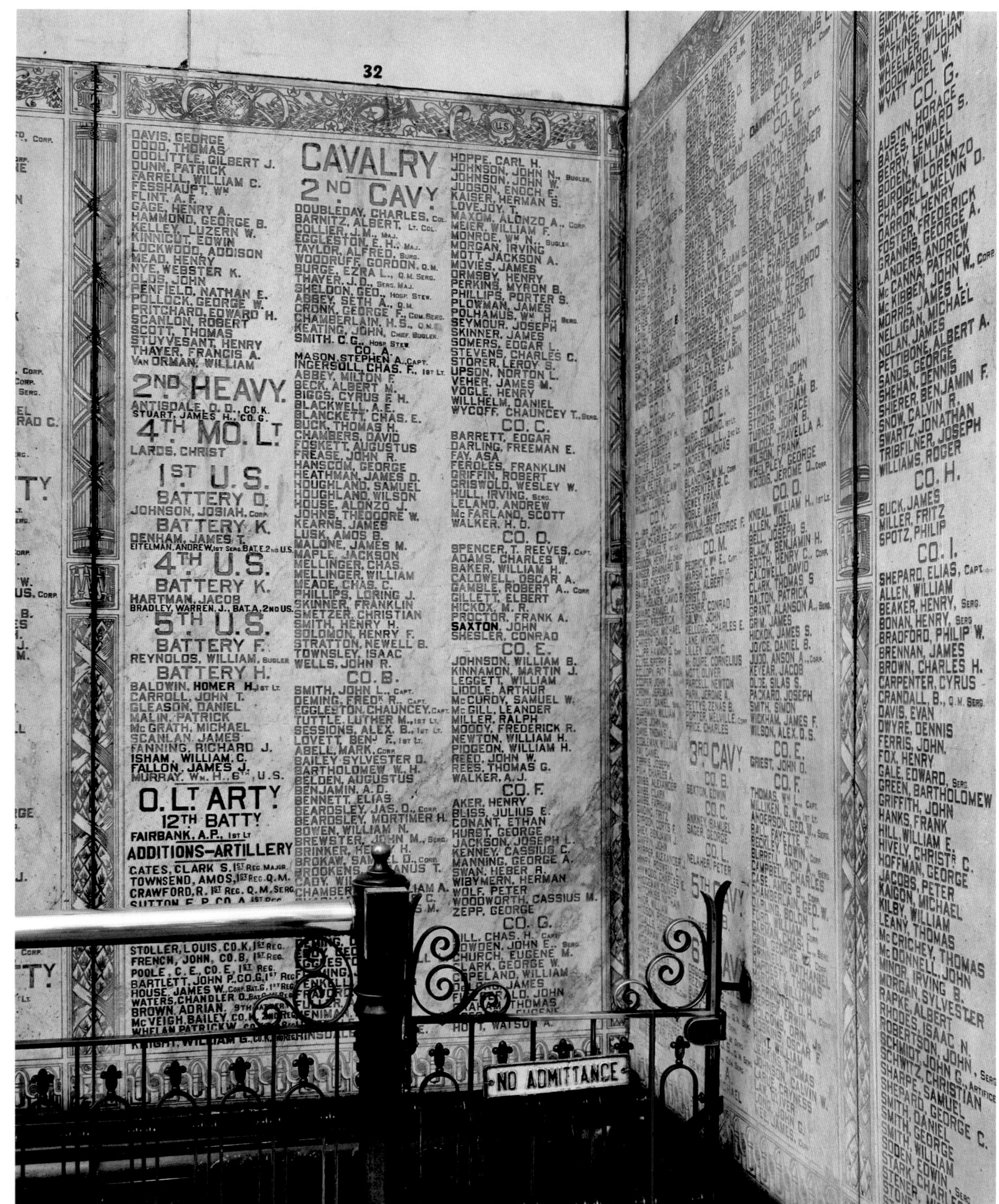

Interior, Cuyahoga County Soldiers and Sailors Monument. Public Square. 1894. Levi T. Scofield, architect-sculptor. March 1988.

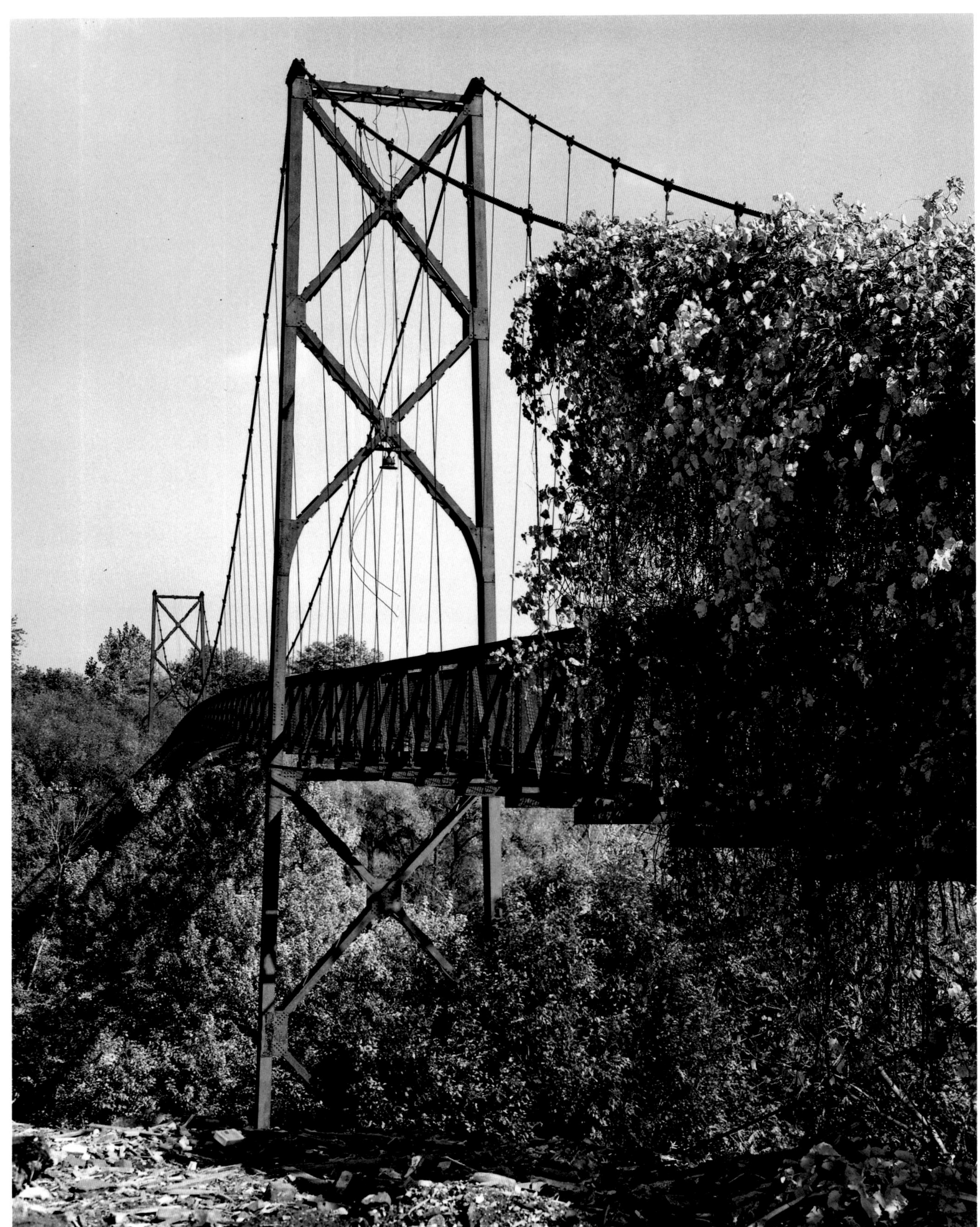

Sidaway Pedestrian Suspension Bridge. Sidaway Road. 1930. Wilbur J. Watson, engineer. October 1987.

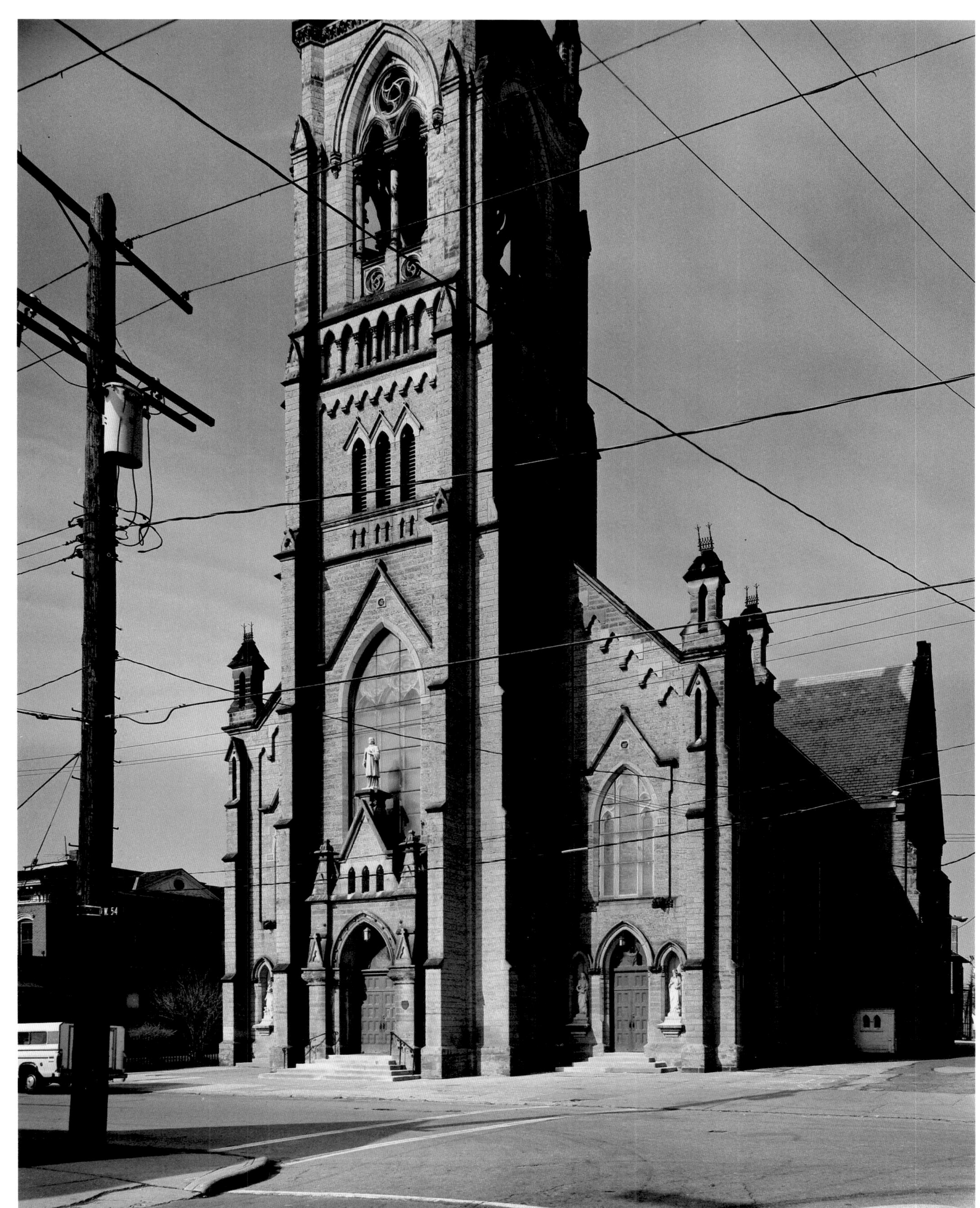

St. Stephen's Roman Catholic Church. 1930 West 54th Street. 1873-81. Cudell and Richardson, architects. April 1989.

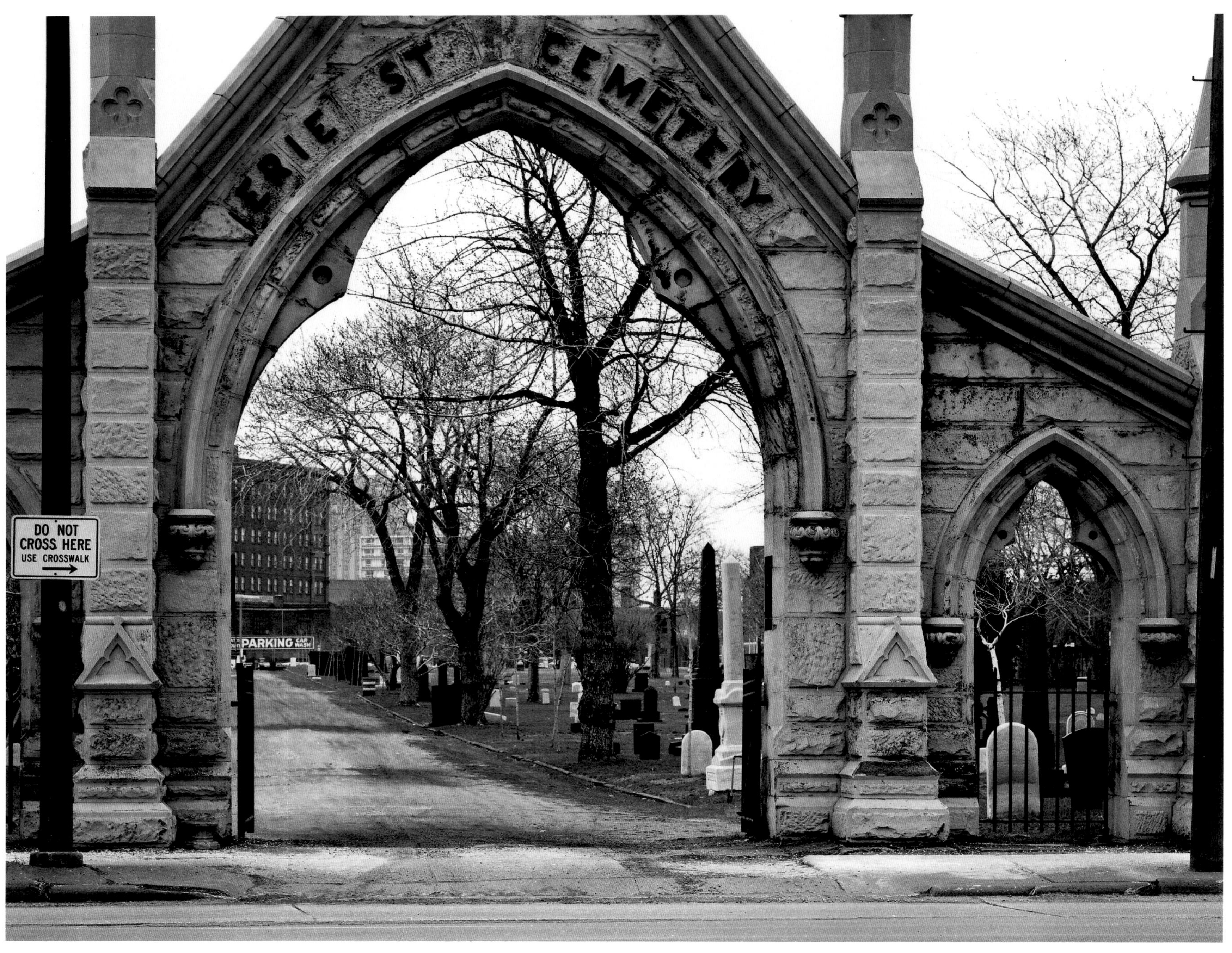

Erie Street Cemetery. Erie and East 9th Streets. Land acquired 1826. Gothic gateway erected 1870. April 1989.

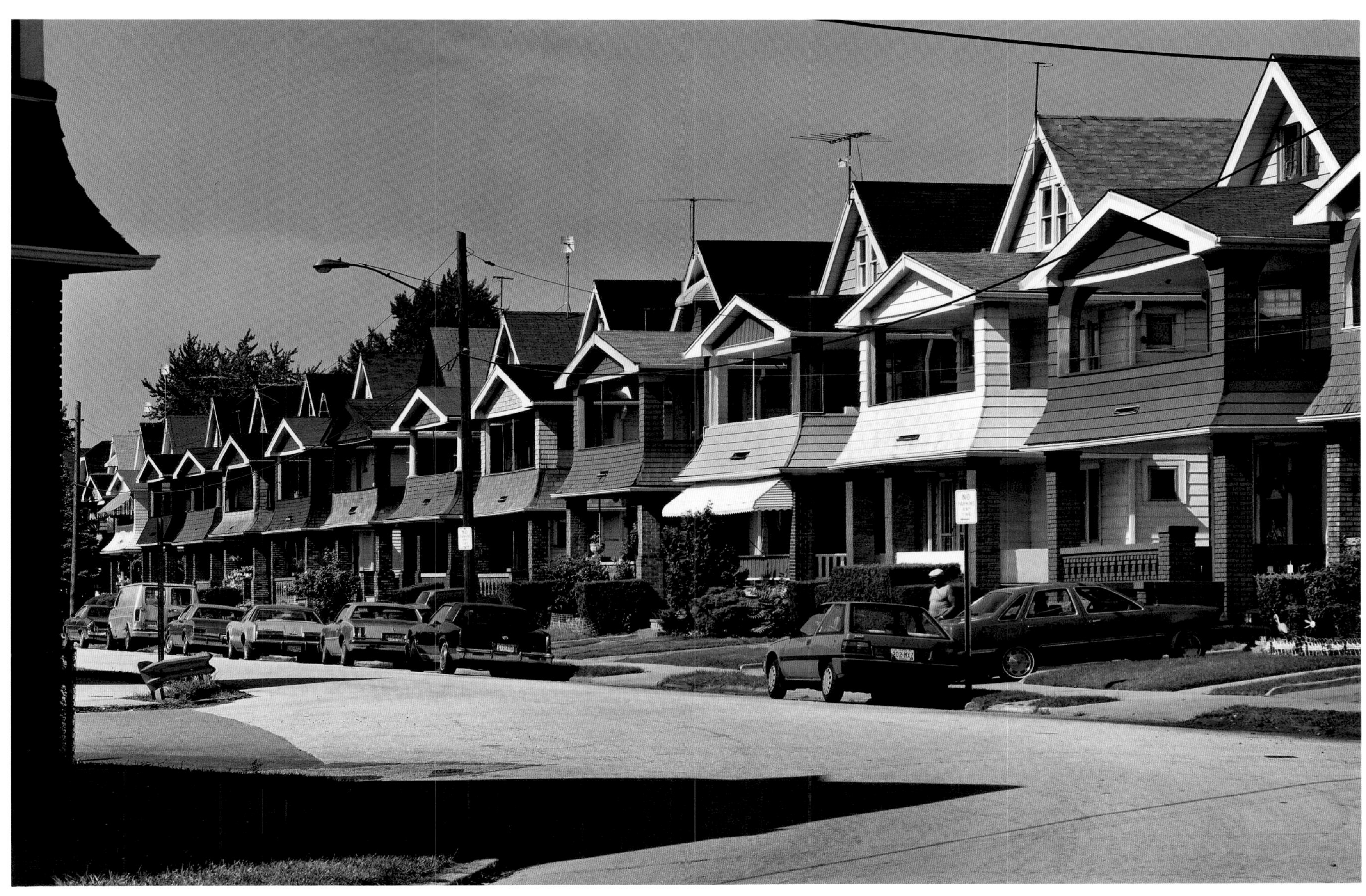

"Cleveland Doubles." East 28th Street and Paxton Road. Built ca. 1915-25. Typical Northeastern Ohio housing. July 1988.

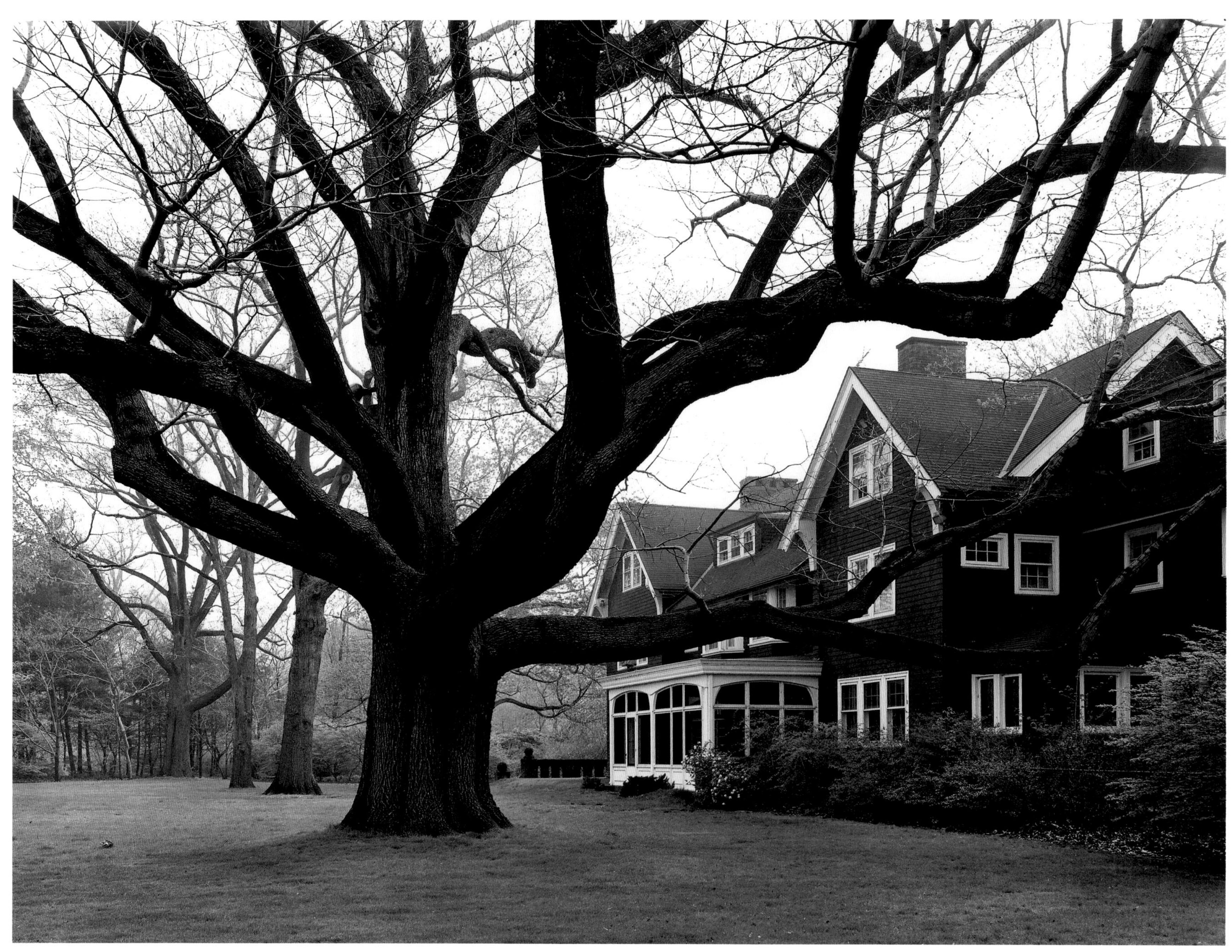

The Great Oak at Katewood (Albert Fairchild Holden Residence). 9511 Lake Shore Boulevard, Bratenahl. Ca. 1898. May 1988.

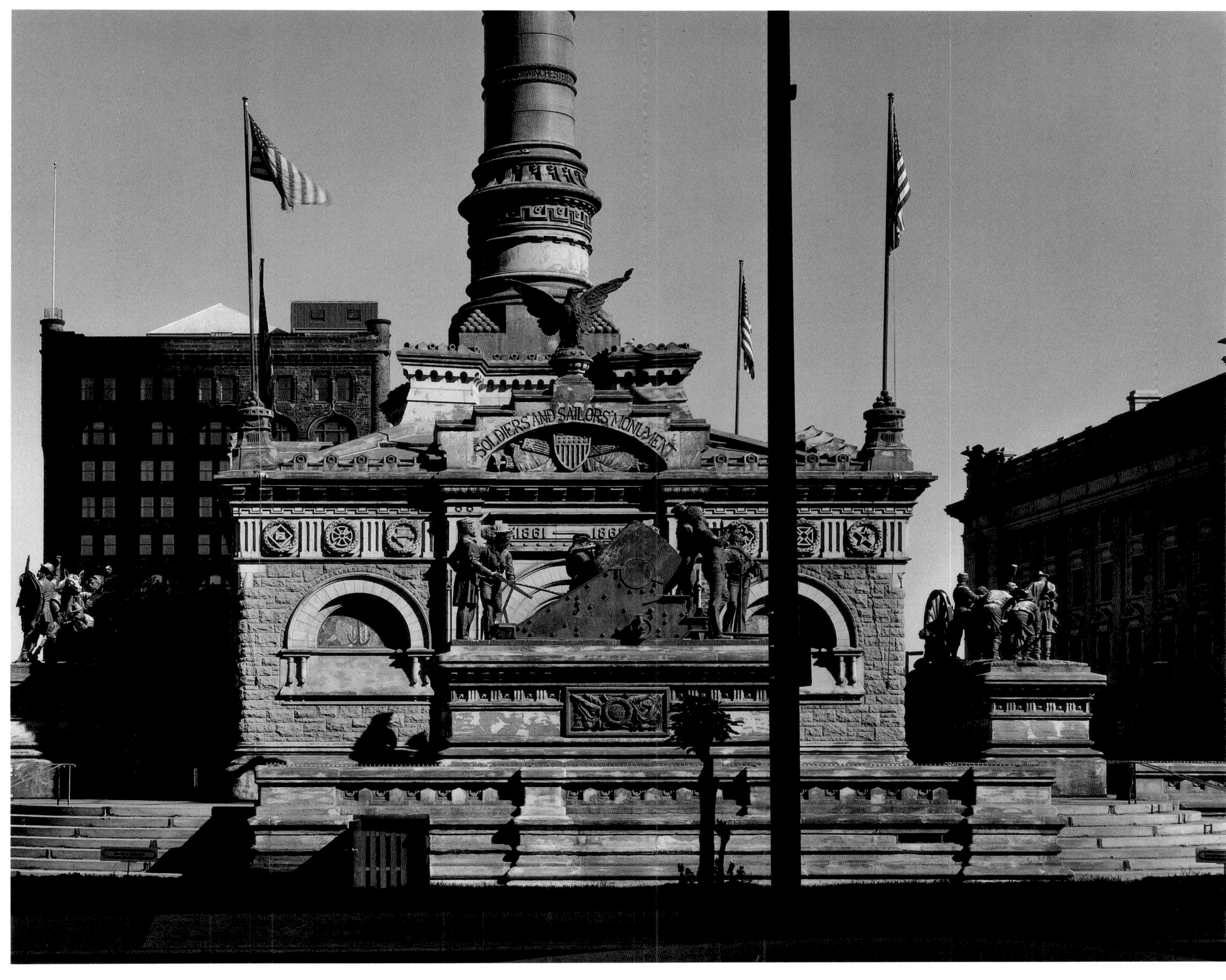

Cuyahoga County Soldiers and Sailors Monument. Public Square. 1894. Levi T. Scofield, architect-sculptor. July 1987.

One would expect a city's architecture to reflect the character and values of its citizenry.

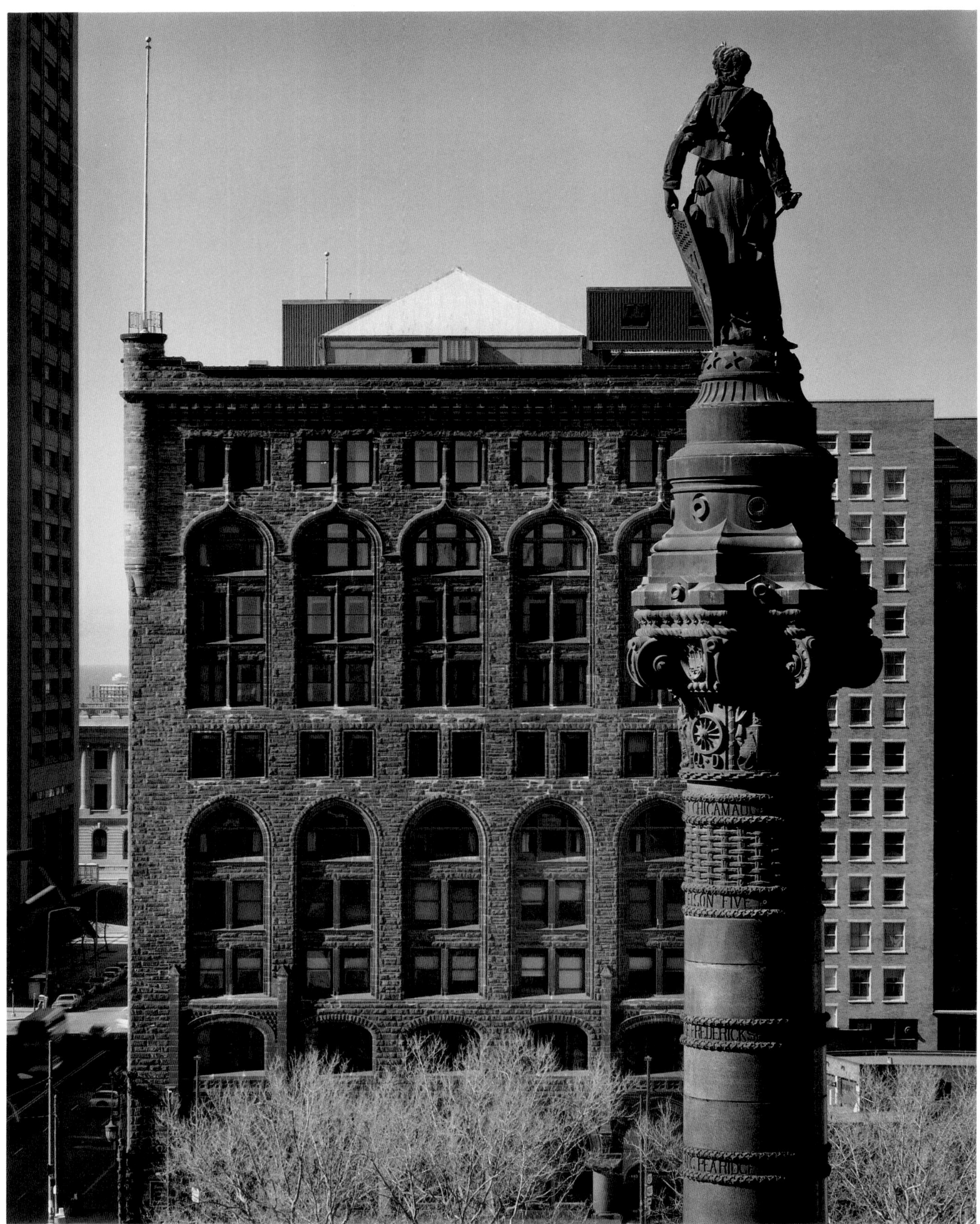

Society National Bank (originally Society for Savings Building). Public Square. 1889. John Wellborn Root, architect. Foreground: Figure of *Liberty* atop the Cuyahoga County Soldiers and Sailors Monument. 1894. Levi T. Scofield, architect-sculptor. March 1988.

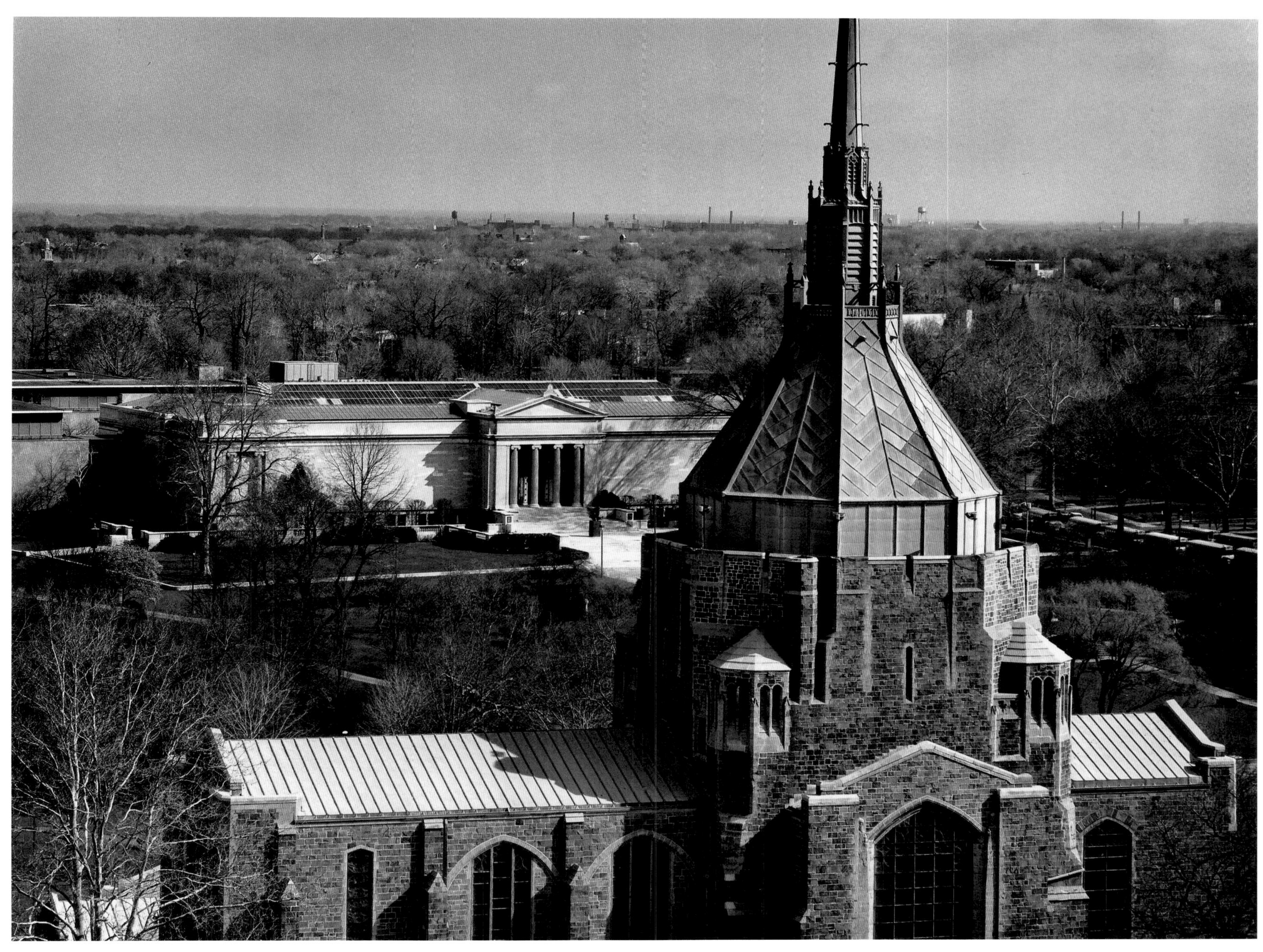

Epworth-Euclid United Methodist Church and The Cleveland Museum of Art. Foreground: Epworth-Euclid United Methodist Church. East 107th Street and Chester Avenue. 1928. Bertram Goodhue, and Walker and Weeks, architects. Background: The Cleveland Museum of Art. 11150 East Boulevard. 1916 Building. Hubbell and Benes, architects. April 1989.

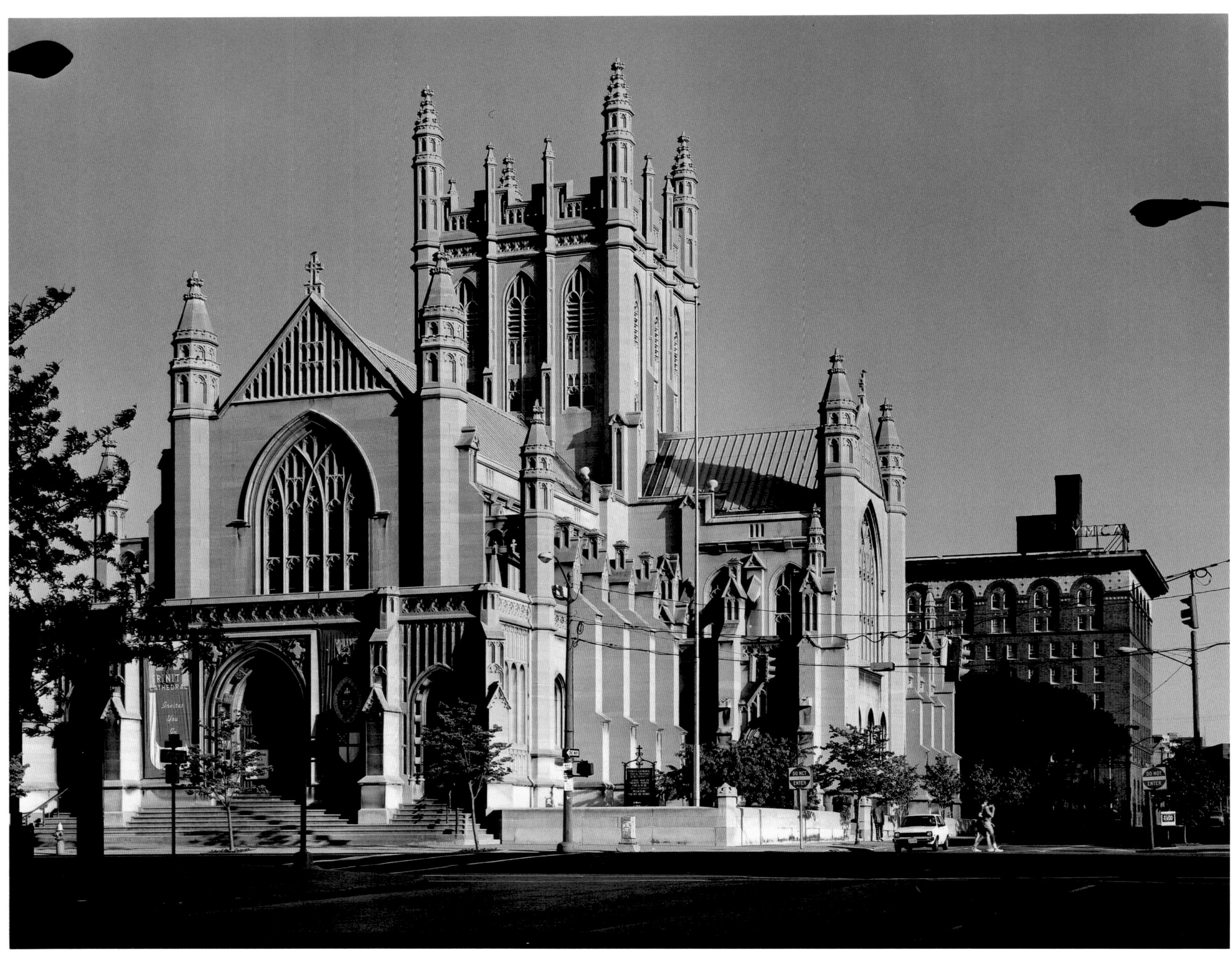

Trinity Cathedral. Euclid Avenue and East 22nd Street. 1907. Charles F. Schweinfurth, architect. May 1988.

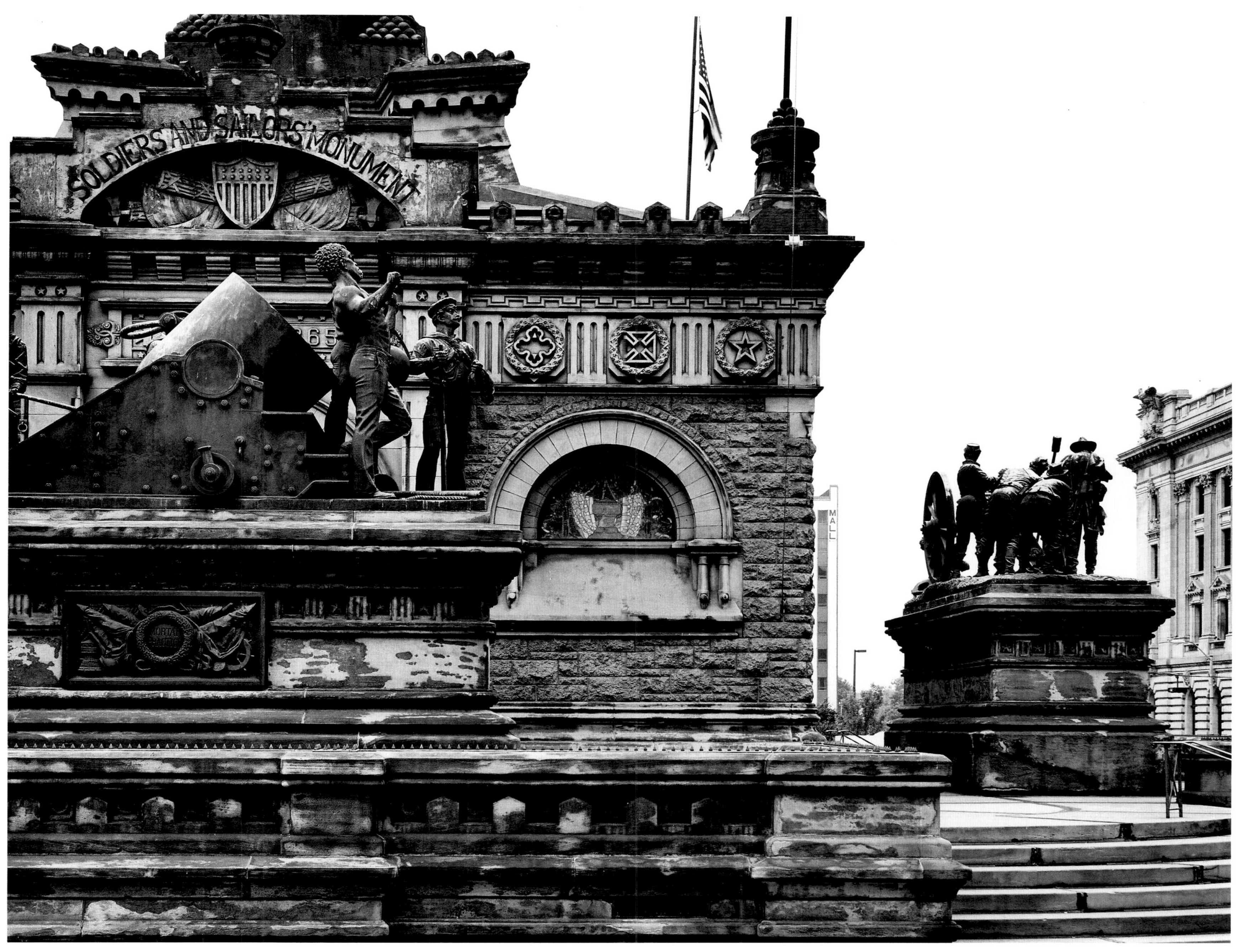

Cuyahoga County Soldiers and Sailors Monument. Public Square. 1894. Levi T. Scofield, architect-sculptor. August 1987.

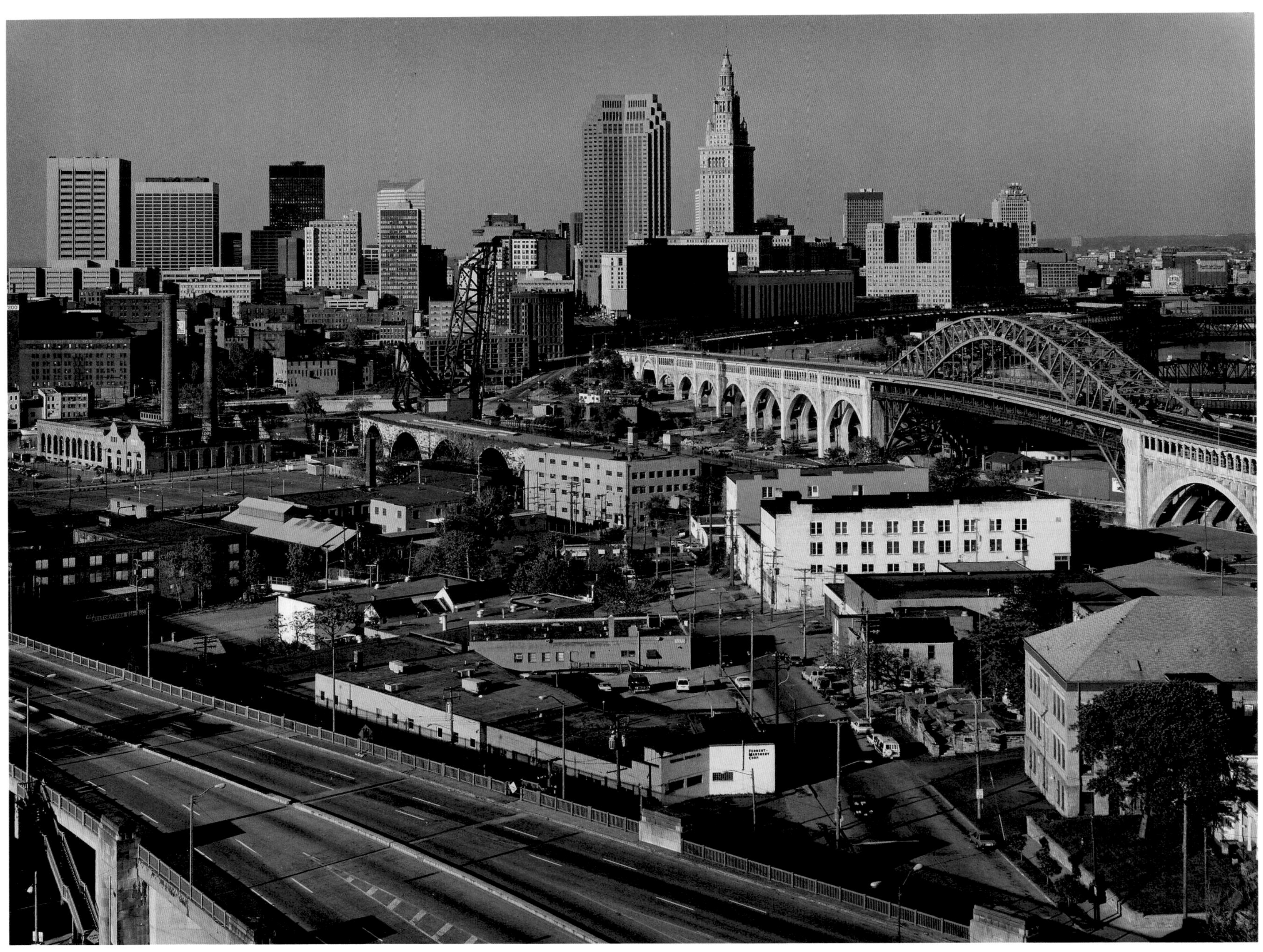

View of the Flats, Detroit-Superior High-Level Bridge, and Downtown Cleveland from an Apartment Building in Ohio City. Detroit-Superior Bridge opened 1918. William A. Stinchcomb, county engineer. May 1988.

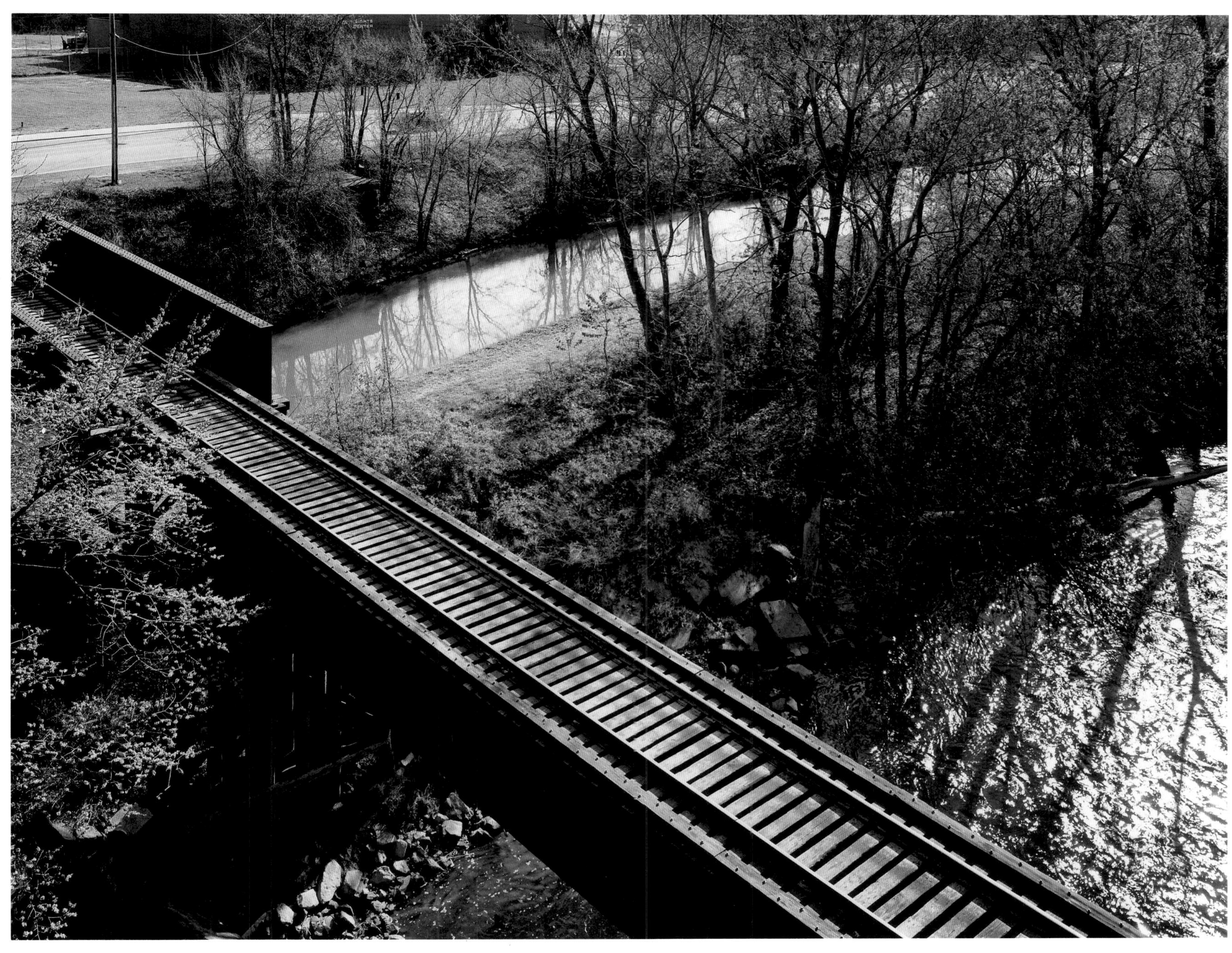

Where the Canal and Cuyahoga River Parallel. Near Canal Road and East 71st Street, Cuyahoga Heights. May 1988.

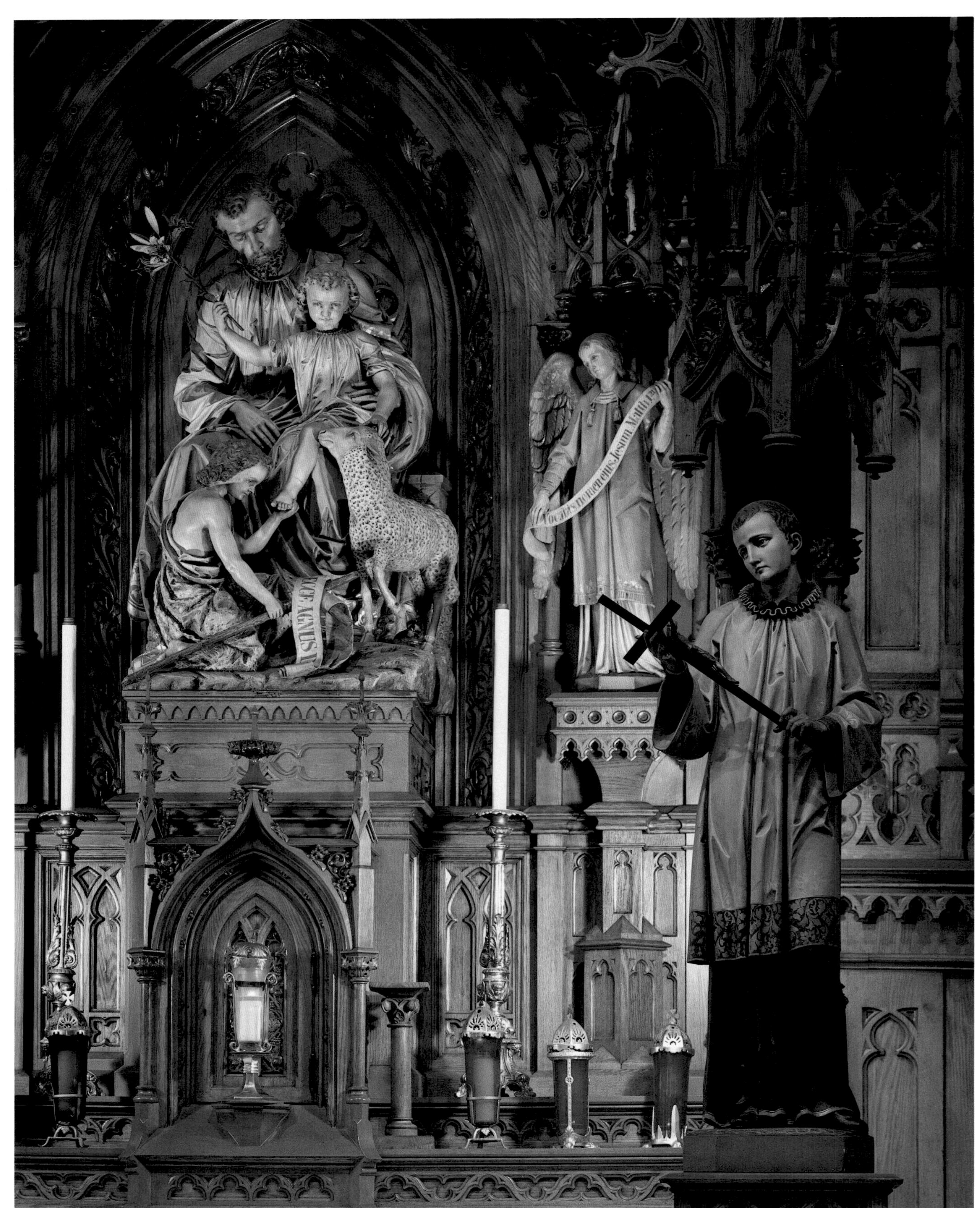

St. Joseph Altar, St. Stephen's Roman Catholic Church. 1930 West 54th Street. 1873-81. Cudell and Richardson, architects. Sculpture imported from Munich, Germany, in 1893. October 1987.

C O N F R O N T A T I O N S

71

73

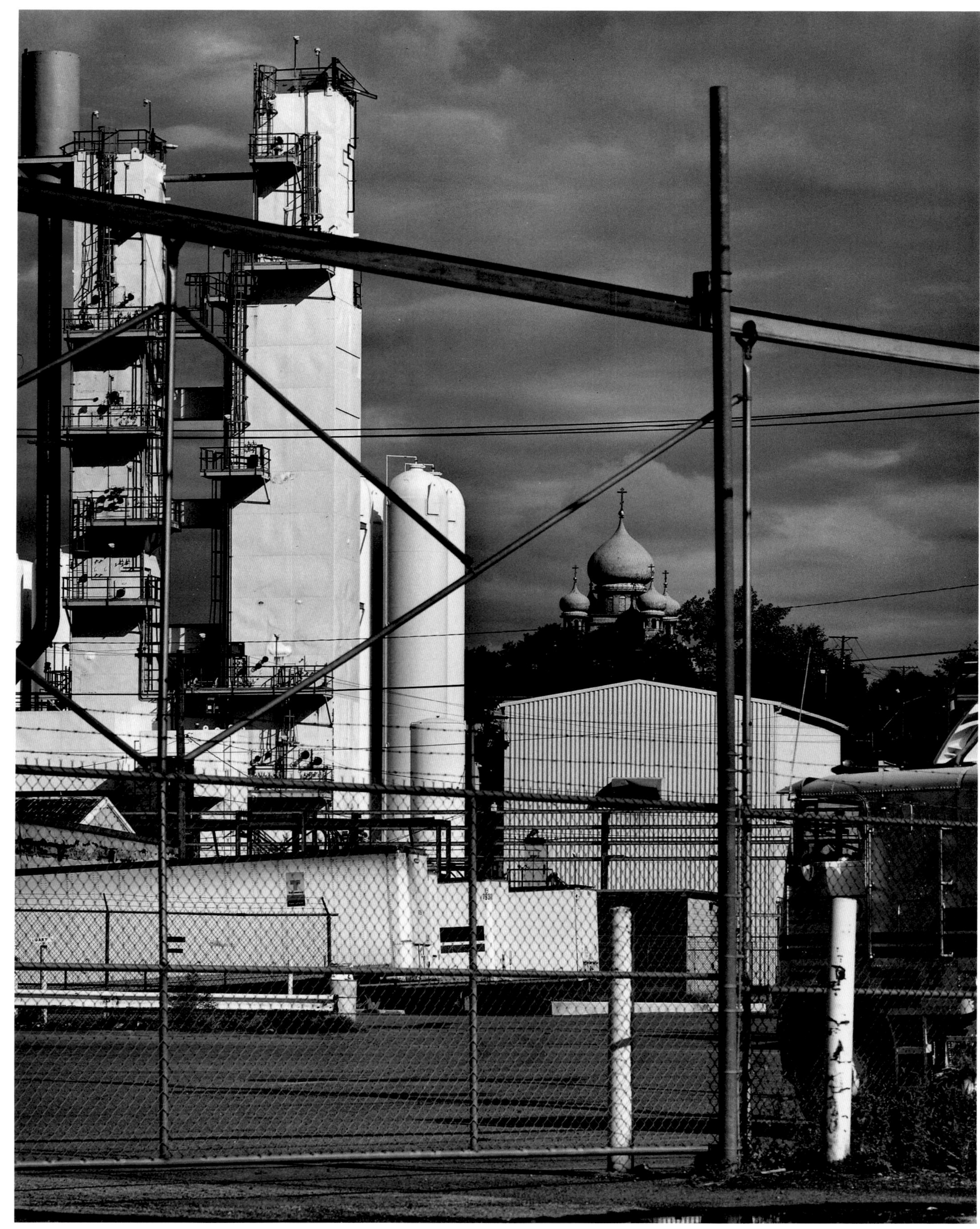

Air Products and Chemicals Inc. Oxygen Plant with Towers of St. Theodosius in Background. Air Products Plant located at 2820 Quigley Road. St. Theodosius located at 2547 St. Tikhon Street. 1912. Frederick C. Baird, architect. October 1987.

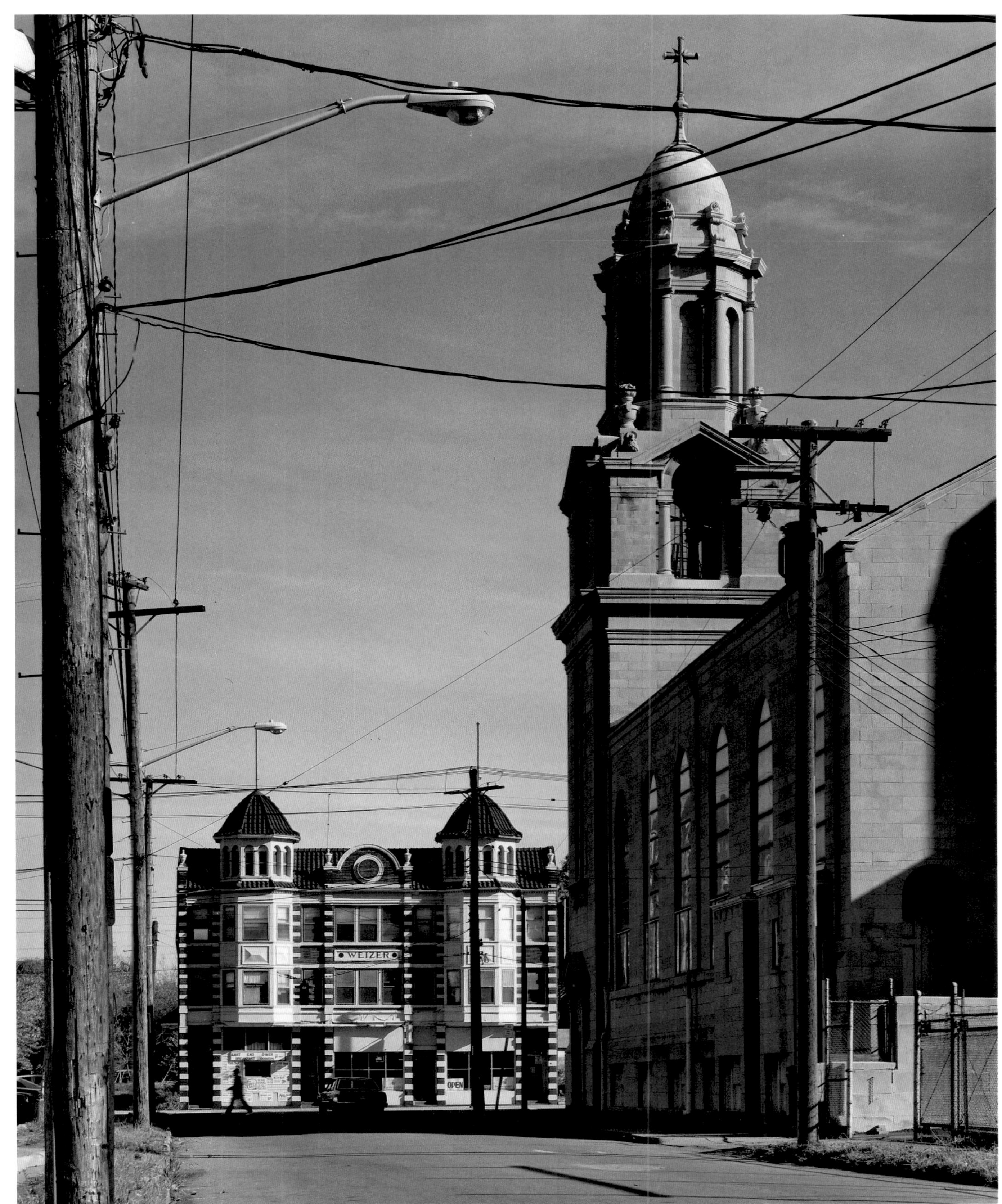

St. Elizabeth of Hungary Church and the Weizer Block. 9016 and 8937 Buckeye Road. 1918-22 and 1913. Both structures by Emile Uhlrich, architect. October 1987.

It is where appositions are direct and unblurred that the camera can describe them clearly.

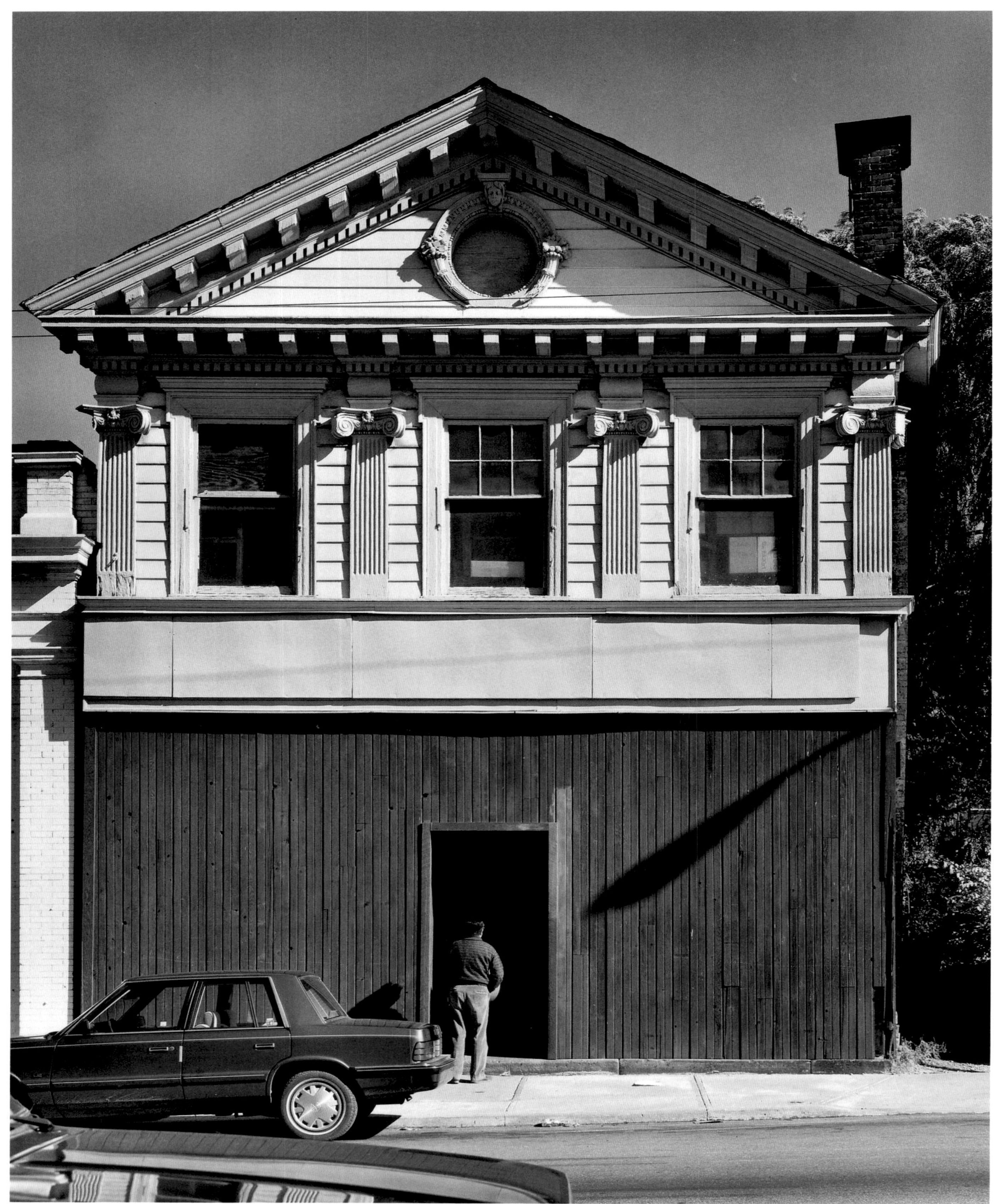

7735 Broadway Avenue.
October 1987.

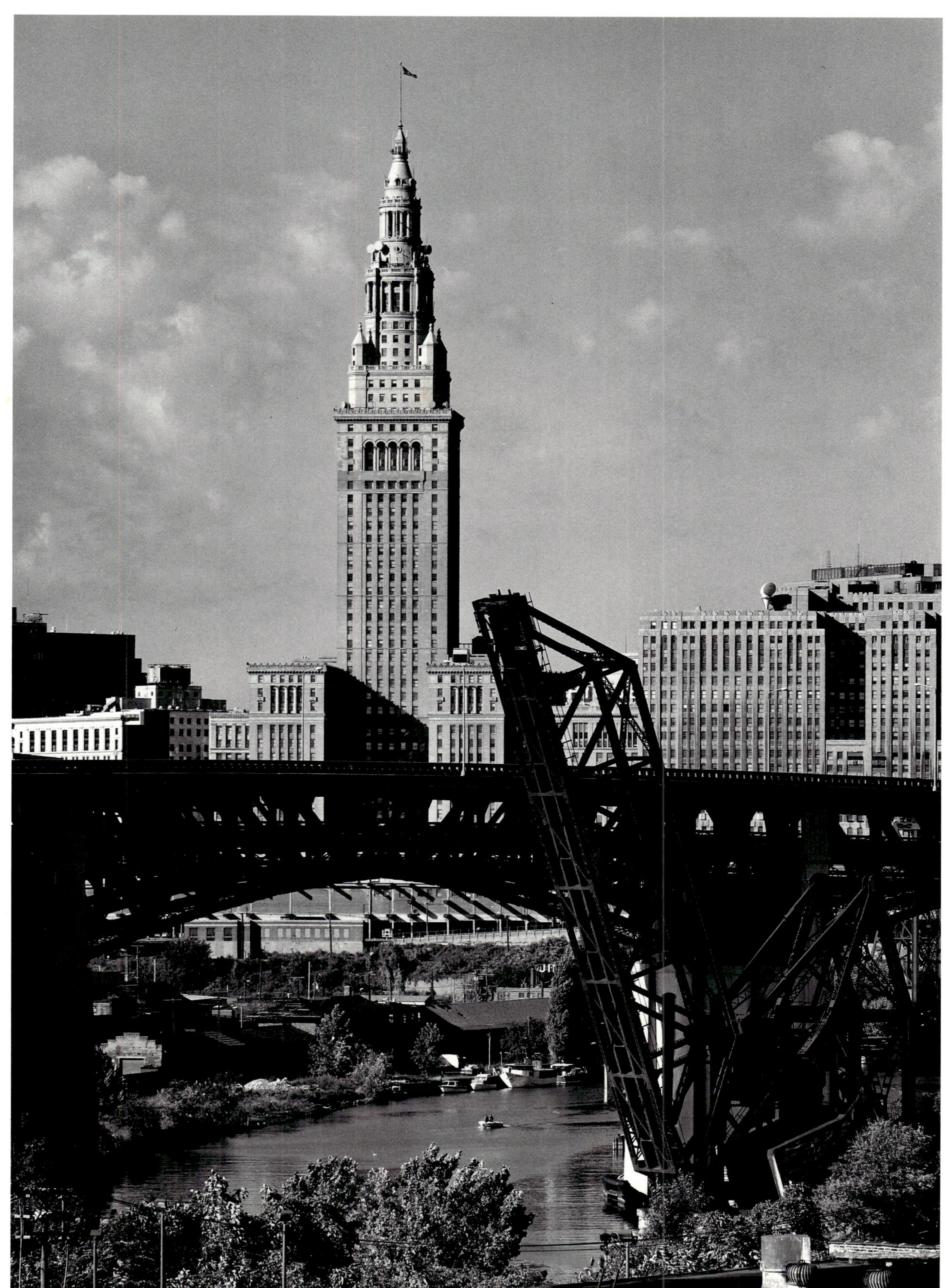

View of Terminal Tower from Abbey Avenue near East 15th Street. Tower completed 1927. Graham, Anderson, Probst, and White, architects. October 1987.

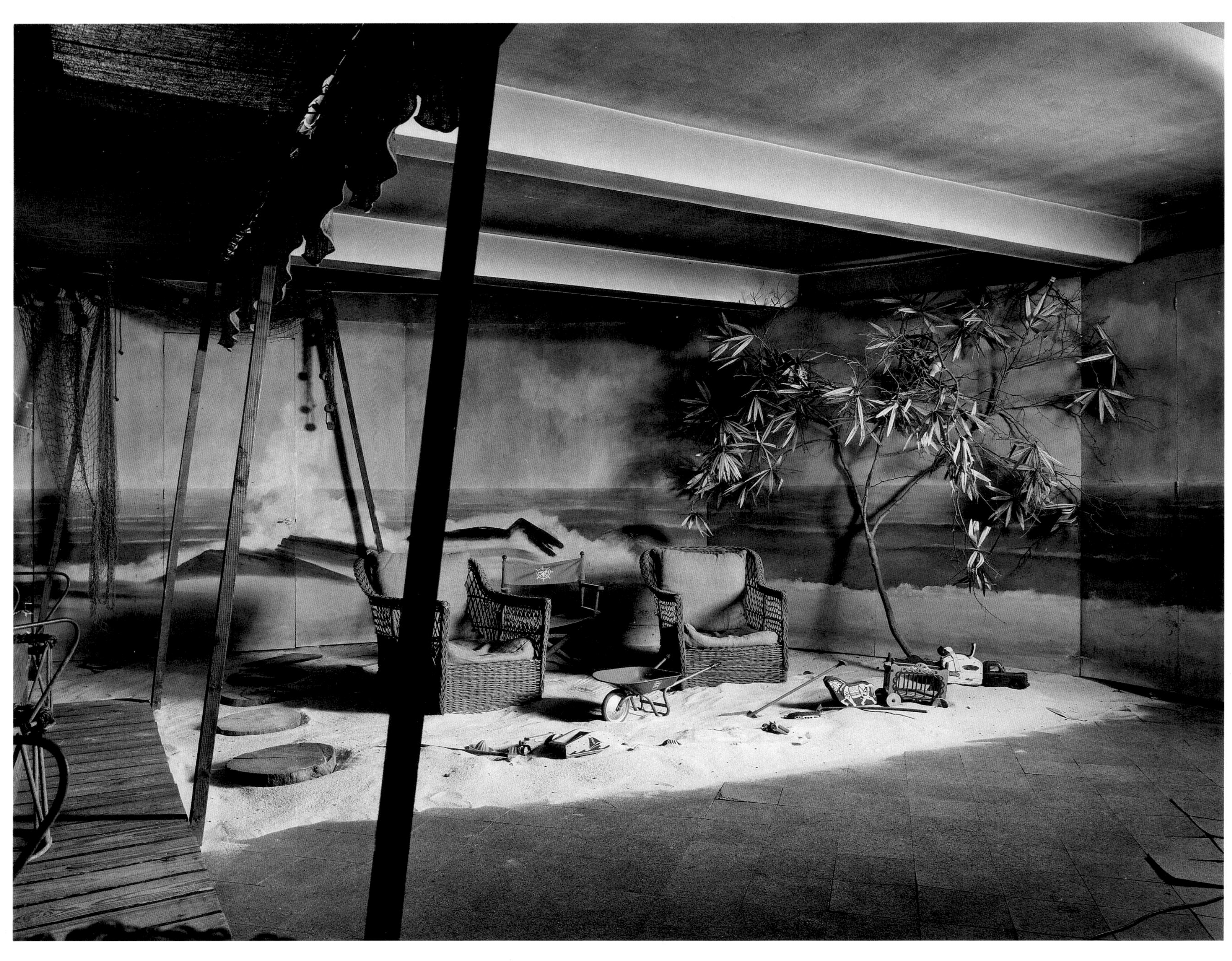

Recreation Room, William G. Mather Residence, "Gwinn." Decorated for "S. S. Gwinn" party in 1951. 1988.

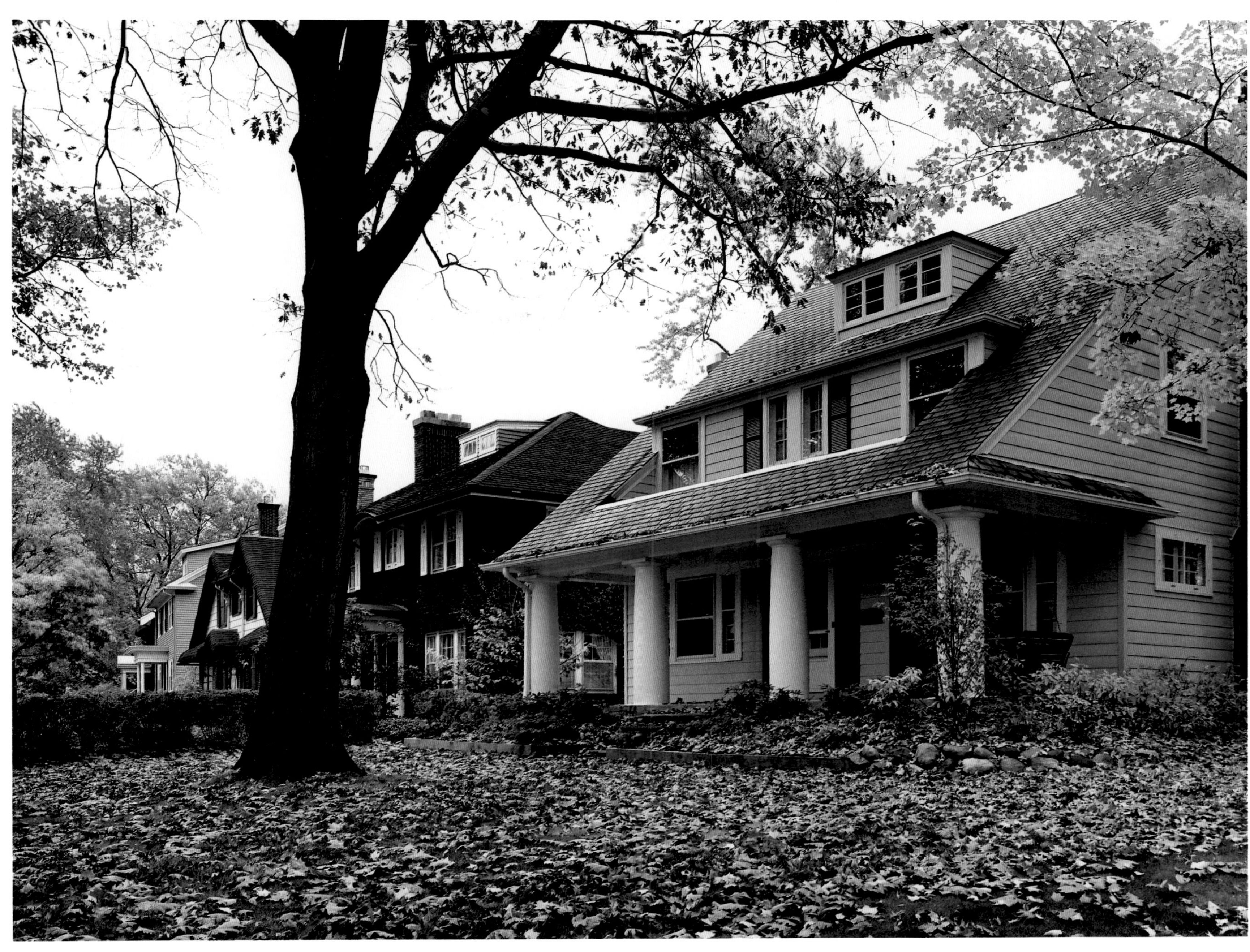

Residence of Mr. and Mrs. Richard Stout. 14406 Drexmore Road, Shaker Heights. Built ca. 1915. October 1987.

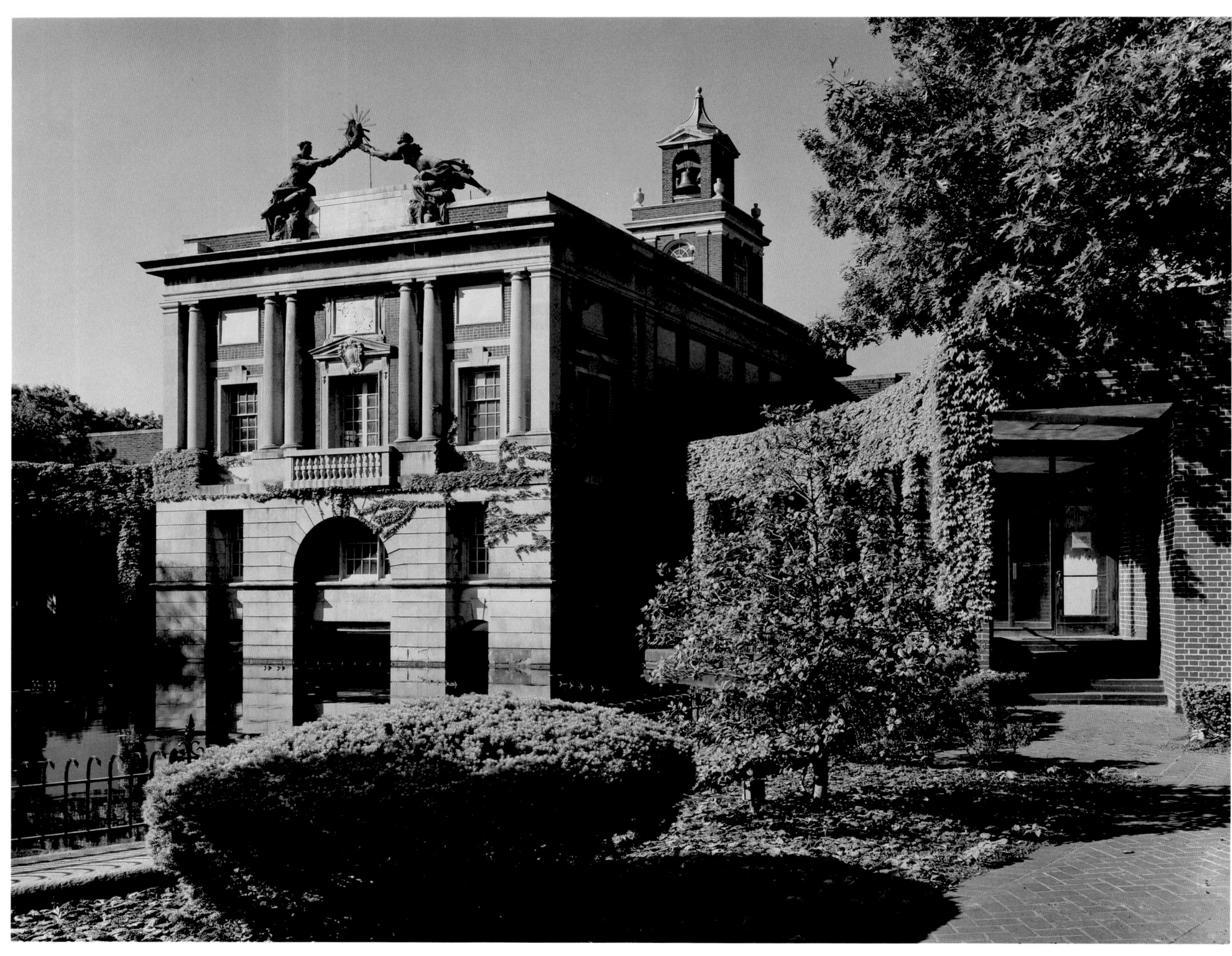

Nela Park Institute. Noble and Terrace Roads, East Cleveland. 1921. Wallis and Goodwillie, architects. May 1988.

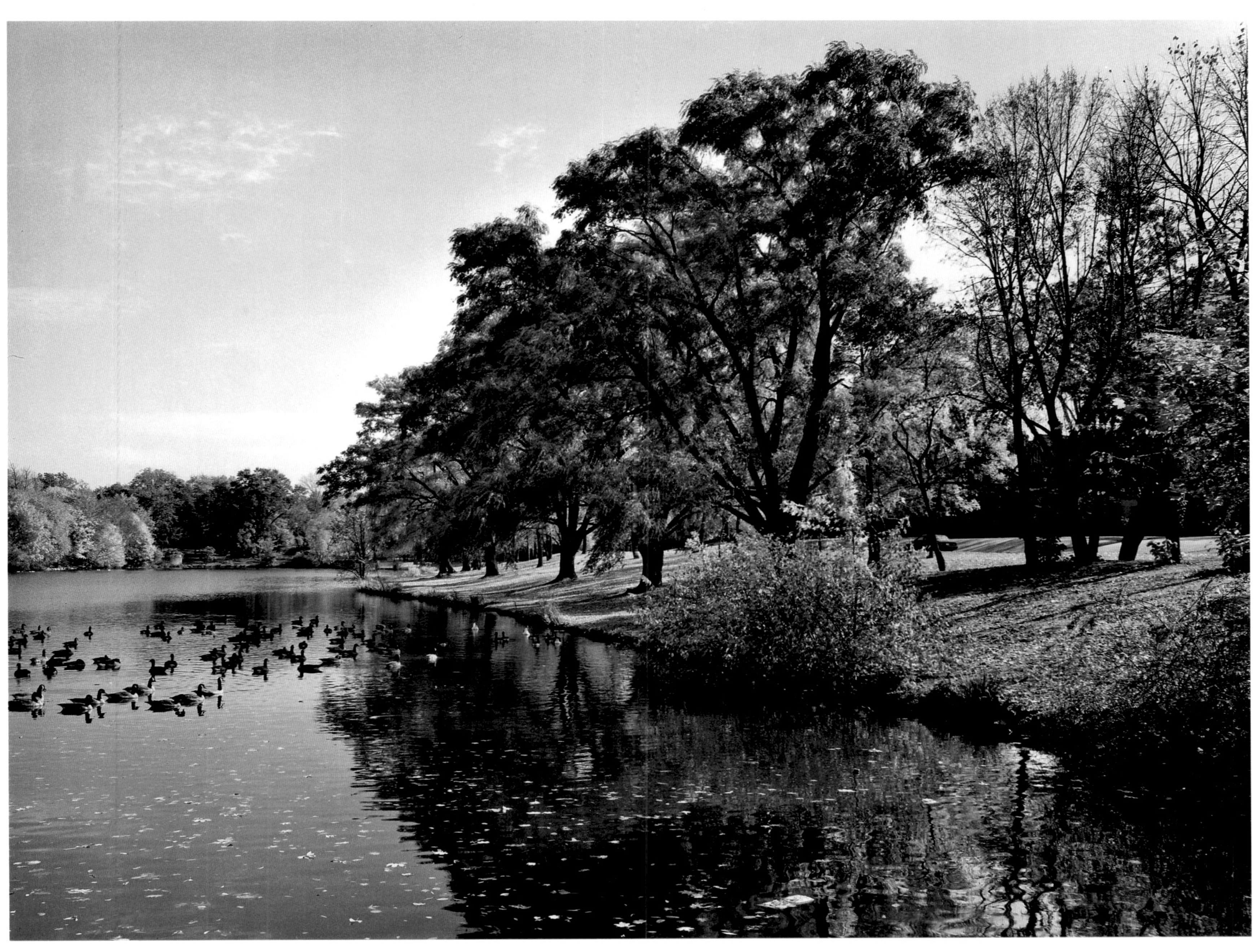

View of Shaker Lakes from Andover Road. Landscaped ca. 1895. Ernest W. Bowditch, landscape architect. October 1987.

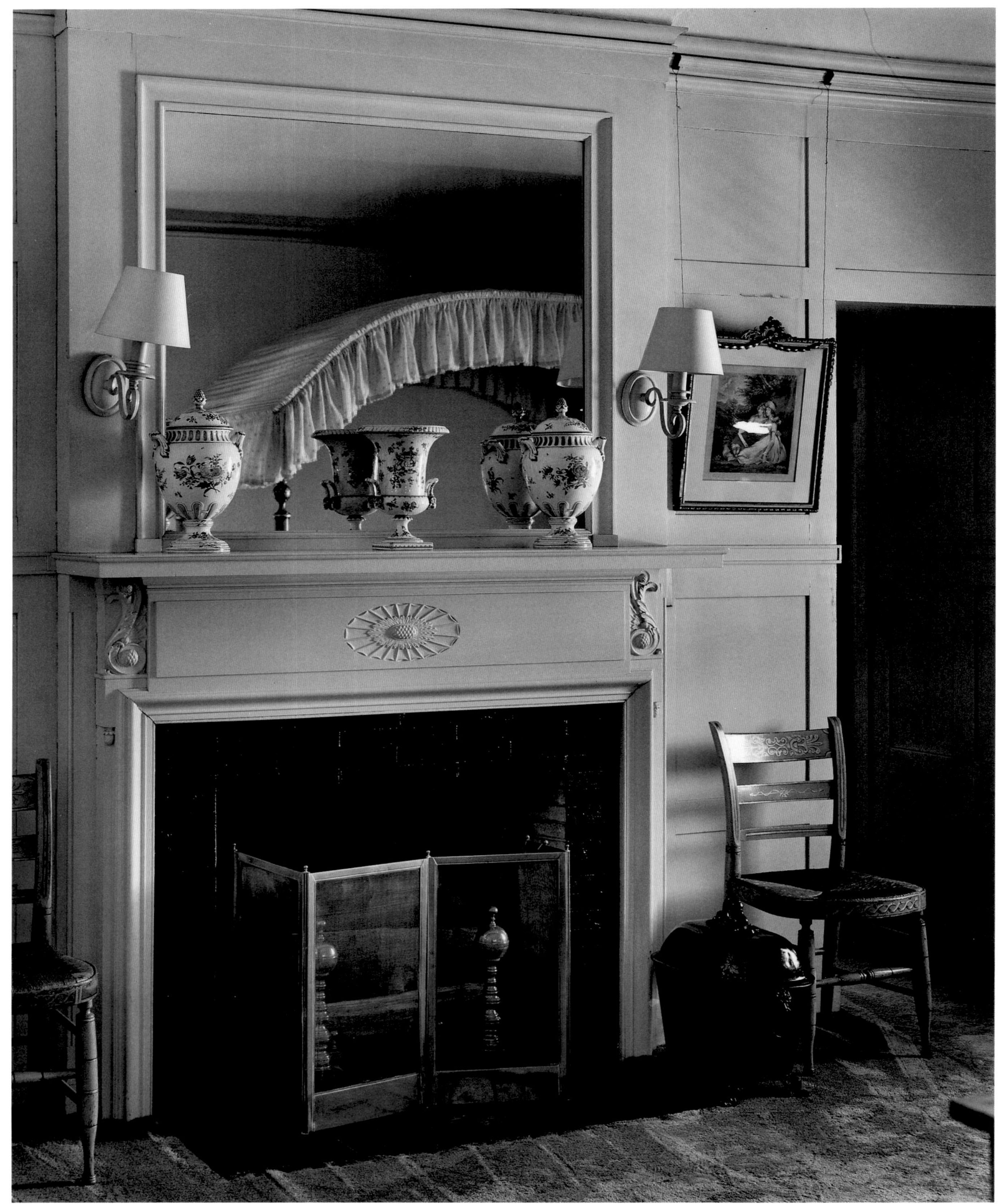

Bedroom, William G. Mather Residence, "Gwinn." 12407 Lake Shore Boulevard, Bratenahl. 1908. Charles Platt, architect. February 1988.

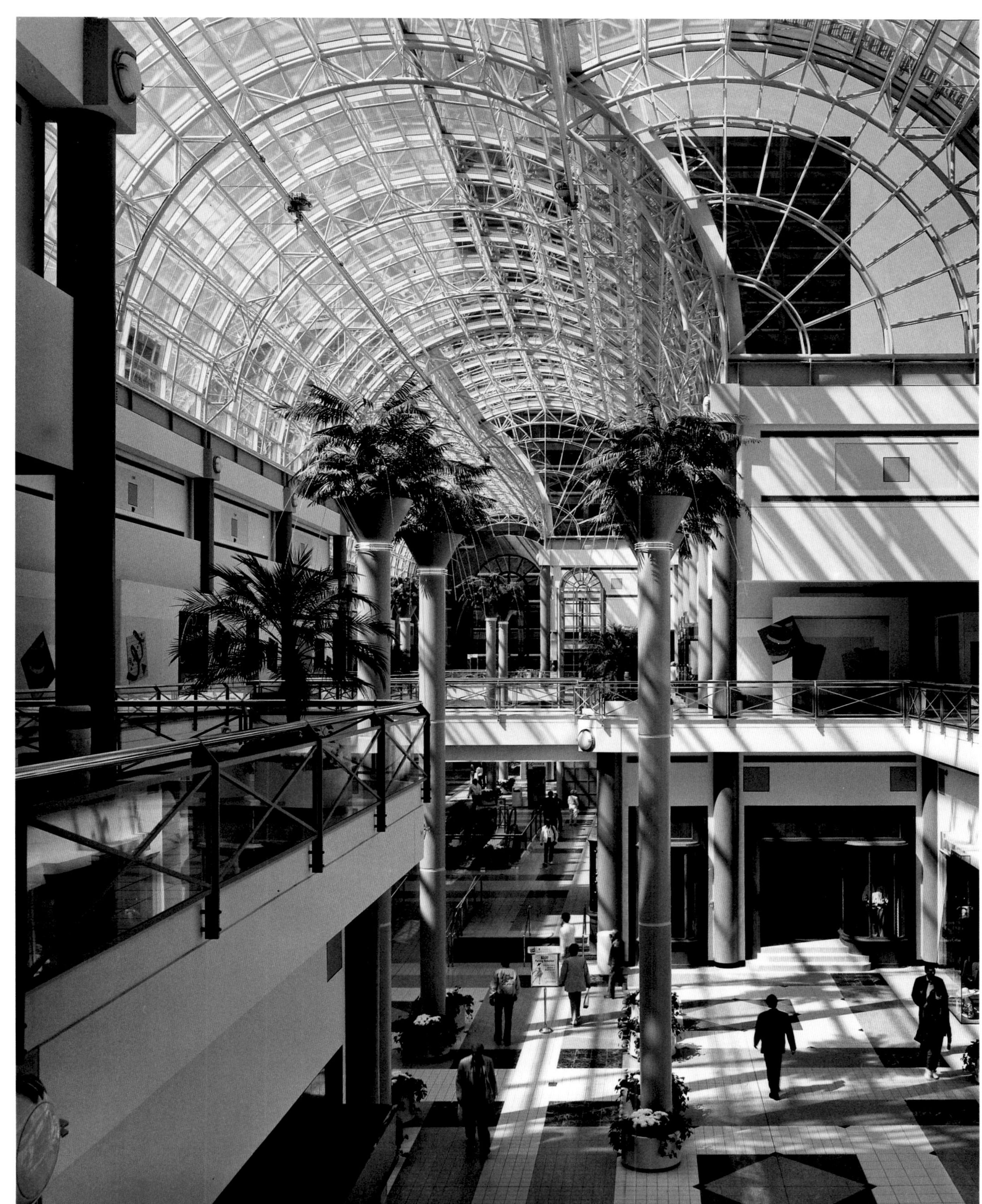

Palm Courts, The Galleria at Erieview. 1301 East 9th Street. 1987. Kober/Belluschi, Associates Inc., architects. May 1988.

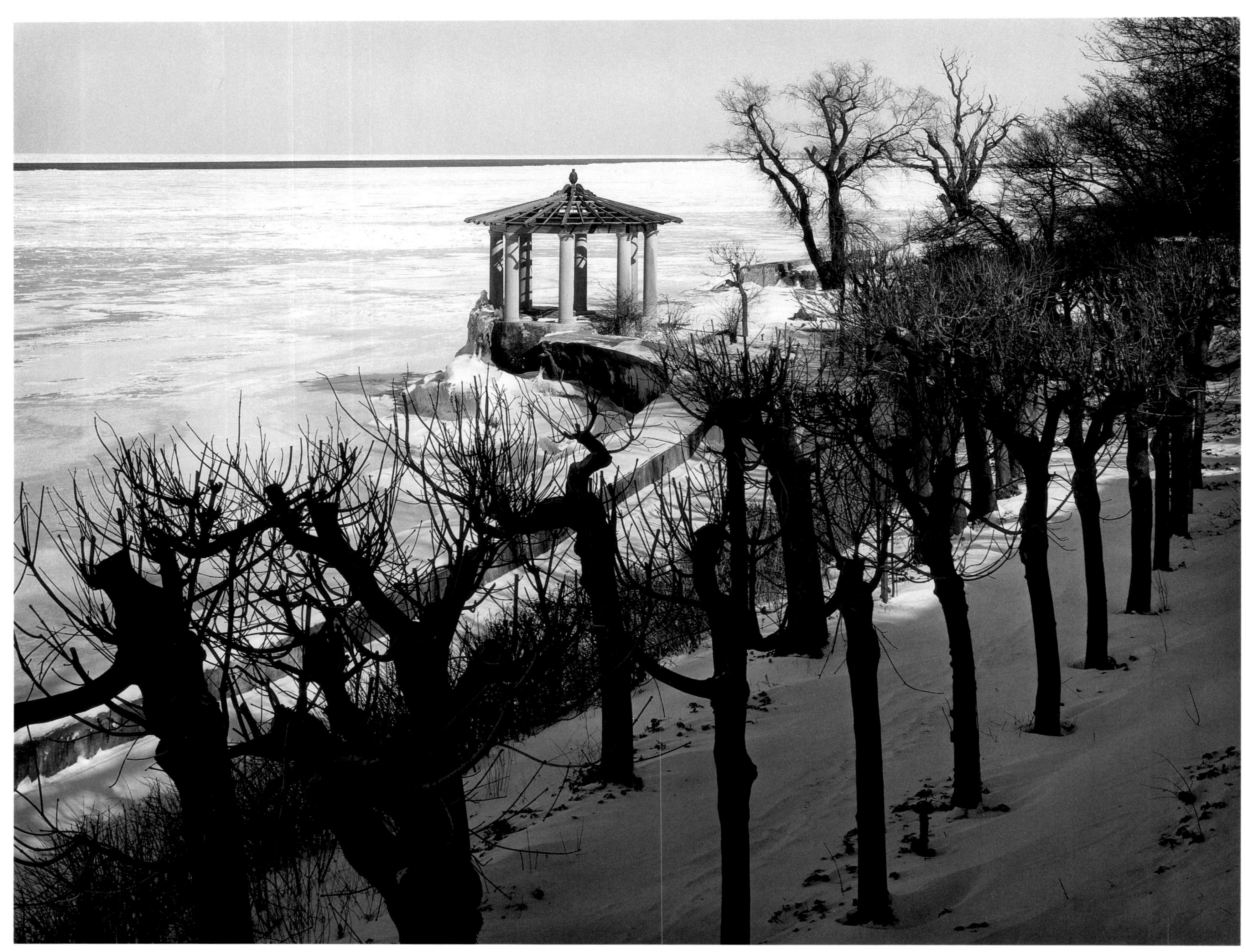

Gazebo, William G. Mather Residence, "Gwinn." 12407 Lake Shore Boulevard, Bratenahl. 1908. Charles Platt, architect. February 1988.

Biography

1928 Born in Boston, Massachusetts
1950 A.B., Harvard University
Lives and works in New York City

Books by Cervin Robinson

Architecture Transformed: A History of the Photography of Buildings from 1839 to the Present, with Joel Herschman, Cambridge, Mass., MIT Press, 1987

Cervin Robinson: Photographs 1958-1983, Wellesley: The Grace Slack McNeil Program in American Art, Wellesley College, 1983

Skyscraper Style: Art Deco New York, with Rosemarie Haag Bletter, New York, Oxford University Press, 1975

Special pictures for *The Architecture of Frank Furness* by James F. O'Gorman, Philadelphia Museum of Art, 1973.

Selected Articles and Photo Essays

''County Courthouse Project: Group Work, Assigned Work,'' *Photograph*, July 1977, 10-13.

''Architectural Photography: Feelies, Data Banks, and a Cult of the Pleasingly Senile,'' *Journal of Architectural Education*, November 1975, 10-15.

''Skyscraper Style: Art Deco New York,'' with Rosemarie Bletter, *Artforum*, November 1974, 30-40.

''Chrysler,'' *Architecture PLUS*, May-June 1974, 50-55

Selected Exhibitions

Landmark Churches, Municipal Art Society, 1984
Retrospective, 1958-1983, Rice University 1983
Landmarks that Aren't, II, Municipal Art Society, 1983
Landmarks that Aren't, I, Municipal Art Society, 1982

Awards

1986 American Institute of Architects Honor Award
1971 Guggenheim Fellowship